D0668854

Circus
Philosophicus

First published by O-Books, 2010
O Books is an imprint of John Hunt Publishing Ltd., The Bothy, Deershot Lodge, Park Lane, Ropley,
Hants, SO24 0BE, UK
office1@o-books.net
www.o-books.net

Distribution in:

UK and Europe
Orca Book Services Ltd
tradeorders@orcabookservices.co.uk
directorders@orcabookservices.co.uk
Tel: 01235 465521 Fax: 01235 465555
Int. code (44)

USA and Canada
NBN
custserv@nbnbooks.com
Tel: 1 800 462 6420 Fax: 1 800 338 4550

Australia and New Zealand
Brumby Books
sales@brumbybooks.com.au
Tel: 61 3 9761 5535 Fax: 61 3 9761 7095

Far East (offices in Singapore, Thailand,
Hong Kong, Taiwan)
Pansing Distribution Pte Ltd
kemal@pansing.com
Tel: 65 6319 9939 Fax: 65 6462 5761

South Africa
Stephan Phillips (pty) Ltd
Email: orders@stephanphillips.com
Tel: 27 21 4489839 Telefax: 27 21 4479879

Text copyright Graham Harman 2009

Design: Stuart Davies

ISBN: 978 1 84694 400 0

All rights reserved. Except for brief quotations
in critical articles or reviews, no part of this
book may be reproduced in any manner without
prior written permission from the publishers.

The rights of Graham Harman as author have
been asserted in accordance with the
Copyright, Designs and Patents Act 1988.

A CIP catalogue record for this book is available
from the British Library.

Printed by CPI Antony Rowe

O Books operates a distinctive and ethical publishing philosophy in
all areas of its business, from its global network of authors to
production and worldwide distribution.

Circus
Philosophicus

Graham Harman

BOOKS

Winchester, UK
Washington, USA

CONTENTS

Biographical Notes

Graham Harman is Associate Vice Provost for Research at the American University in Cairo, Egypt, where he has taught philosophy since 2000. He lives on an island in the Nile in the Zamalek neighborhood, the source of his online name "doctorzamalek." (His widely read philosophy blog can be found at http://doctorzamalek2.wordpress.com/ .) So far he has survived two close brushes with death: struck by downed electrical cable in Chicago in 1992, and attacked by a rabid Egyptian dog in 2008.

Harman is a sixth-generation native of Iowa and a former Chicago sportswriter. In 2006 he co-founded the Speculative Realism movement in philosophy (with Ray Brassier, Iain Hamilton Grant, and Quentin Meillassoux), and in 2009 the Object-Oriented Ontology splinter faction of the movement (with Ian Bogost and Levi Bryant).

Other Books by Graham Harman
Tool-Being: Heidegger and the Metaphysics of Objects
(Chicago: Open Court, 2002)
Guerrilla Metaphysics: Phenomenology and the Carpentry of Things (Chicago: Open Court, 2005)
Heidegger Explained: From Phenomenon to Thing
(Chicago: Open Court, 2007)
Prince of Networks: Bruno Latour and Metaphysics
(Melbourne: re.press, 2009)

Forthcoming from zer0 Books
Towards Speculative Realism: Essays and Lectures (2010)
The Quadruple Object (2010)
The Prince and the Wolf: Latour and Harman at the LSE (with Bruno Latour and Peter Erdélyi) (2010)

Weird Realism: Lovecraft and Philosophy (2011)

Forthcoming from Other Publishers

L'objet quadruple, translated from the English by Olivier Dubouclez (Paris: Presses Universitaires de France, 2010)

Meillassoux: Philosophy in the Making (Edinburgh; Edinburgh University Press, 2011)

Treatise on Objects (Ann Arbor, MI: Open Humanities Press, 2011)

1

The Ferris Wheel

Imagine a gigantic ferris wheel of many miles in diameter. The wheel would be lodged in a massive trench in the earth, with the hub at ground level. At all times half of the wheel would be above ground and half beneath the surface. Over the course of twelve or fourteen hours, the wheel would make a complete circuit high in the air and deep beneath the soil. It would carry thousands of separate cars, each of them loaded with various objects. Some would contain printed documents, or zinc and molybdenum Buddhas. Others would be loaded with colorful flags, electric generators, reptiles and birds, miniature explosive charges, bottles of wine, tap dancers, brass bands playing military music, and other entities circling day and night. We will suppose the wheel itself to be made of an unknown and indestructible material not affected by anything that happens in the myth.

The reader should pause and fix this image firmly in mind: a giant rotating wheel, carrying thousands of beings in a long arc ascending to the clouds and vanishing into the darkness of the earth. Let it spin dozens of times in your mind before we move on from this beautiful spectacle. Imagine the faint machinic whirr of its concealed engine, the creaking of its bolts, and the varied sounds emitted by the objects riding in its cars: from neighing horses to mournful woodwind ensembles. Imagine too the ominous mood in the vicinity as its cars plunge deep into the earth. Picture the wheel loaded with animals, bombs, and religious icons. Picture it creaking under the weight of its cargo and emitting a ghostly light as it spins along its colossal circuit. Imagine the artists and engineers of genius who designed such a thing. And consider the human culture that would arise nearby, with the wheel as its sacred point of reference.

• • •

We now add a few new elements to the myth of the ferris wheel, burning the image ever more deeply into the reader's mind. Above ground thousands of people would live in the vicinity of the wheel: some applauding it, others terrified by the sight, with a few insensitive souls bored by the wheel as by a commonplace. Some of the residents would observe its rotations minutely through binoculars, while others would go about their business with no more than occasional glances at the machine. A number of dogs would bark angrily at the wheel, and crows or eagles would sometimes approach for a closer look.

We might stipulate further that numerous chambers have been constructed along the underground path of the wheel. Every ten feet its cars would pass by one of these dimly lit spaces. Some of the underground rooms are filled with people, while others house devices of various sorts. It should be clear that the objects inhabiting each of these rooms will react with especial intensity only to *some* of the entities riding in the wheel. For instance, one of the rooms would be occupied by the members of a secret society or labor union. They have perhaps assembled for a celebration, but with strict orders to wait calmly and quietly until the special flag of their group passes by. When at last it does, they cheer wildly and erupt into violent revelry. There are poets writing verse in some of the rooms, their moods affected deeply by all of the objects, but especially by the various musical groups that circle past. As they hear the music passing their chambers, the character of their poems is altered by what they hear.

A few more examples will clarify the upheavals brought about by the rotation of the wheel. Some of the rooms contain rabid dogs that bark at all passing objects, but especially at the cats and foxes that sometimes circle by, pushing the dogs toward a state of frenzy. Another room is a holding cell for a condemned prisoner, who endures additional torment as portraits of deceased family members pass. Let's suppose as well that one of these underground chambers contains the main power generator for the town above. From time to time a huge electromagnetic coil circles past this room, disrupting the town's energy supply for several minutes, though the wheel continues to circle through an alternate source of power whose nature need not concern us. Whenever this disruption occurs, the observers milling in the streets begin to curse and lament, forgetting the wheel until power is restored and life returns to what it was.

With the exception of the eternal wheel itself, each of the entities in this myth faces a certain degree of danger. After all, some of the cars contain explosive devices; no one knows when or how powerfully they might detonate. If these explode while transiting underground, the chambers closest to them will be annihilated without hope of survivors. If the bombs explode while circling in the air, then so much the worse: for in this case they rain lethal debris over the entire town. Yet the danger also works in reverse, with some of the underground rooms posing a threat to the objects riding the wheel. For instance, a number of the subterranean rooms might be equipped with dormant furnaces. Most of the time these will be inactive. But at sporadic intervals and random temperatures, jets of flame suddenly erupt from the room toward the car that is passing by, spraying fire on whatever entity it contains. Occasionally the flames are hot enough to melt even the metallic images of the Buddha loaded in some of the cars.

Finally it is clear that the rotating objects will have a profound effect on the crowd in the streets, harming or pleasing them on various occasions. The higher the objects move toward the summit of the wheel, the less visible they are to the townspeople. But when they first emerge from the earth, and again when descending to a point near the ground, they are recognized even by children. Indeed, children would surely assemble near the entry and exit points of the wheel, delighted by the sudden emergence or disappearance of surprising things. Each of the objects riding the wheel has a potentially serious impact upon local morale. Some strike the townspeople as comical, provoking sarcastic remarks. Others are melancholy reminders of human frailty: a lonely skull, or the portrait of a reviled former statesman. At such moments the mood in the streets veers toward the tense and the somber. But some of the objects strike different people in different ways, as when a whining kitten circles past, provoking mockery in some and empathy in others. There will also be moments when heavy explosives pass by: these are frightening times for even the most hardened cynics in the town. Some of the cars might also contain loudspeakers emitting religious or political messages. A few observers take these messages seriously and plan conversion or revolution, while others dismiss them with a wave of the hand.

This image of a revolving wheel is a picture of our world. In it, the dramatic interplay of object and network becomes visible. Countless entities circle into and out of our lives, some of them threatening and others ludicrous. The objects in the cars and those on the ground or in the chambers affect one another, coupling and uncoupling from countless relations— seducing, ignoring, ruining, or liberating each other. This process is anything but a game: in it, our accident. The example can be pushed further by imagining that some of the cars contain subatomic particles, and that several underground rooms are able to split these tiny things by channeling powerful beams into their midst, even though no one is watching.

For those who feel distracted by such bizarre examples, more prosaic scenarios are possible. We can assume that the entire complex of underground chambers has been shut down, all of them decommissioned and filled with cement. This having been done, the objects riding the wheel have nothing to hope for and nothing to fear when underground. They do nothing but circle, orbiting forever down into the earth and up into the sky. But even here there is a sense in which the objects change. If nothing else, they will tend to become cold at the top of the wheel as they approach the jet stream, but hot and moist at the bottom as they descend through their dank underground channel. Moreover, their relations with everything found in the outer landscape will change continually, depending on how high or low they are at any moment. These changes are real, and describe vastly different events. A zinc Buddha at the top of the wheel is involved in a different set of relations from the same zinc Buddha at the bottom. The fact that these statues never remain in one place for long does not mean that their specific position at any moment is of less importance than the timeless metal of which they are forged.

This concludes part one of the myth of the wheel. So far, I have used this image to *defend* the model of reality presented by such philosophers as Alfred North Whitehead and Bruno Latour, who focus on the pervasive interrelations of things and discount the existence of entities outside their effects. There is surely some truth in this standpoint, since it is difficult to think of an object apart from the varied relations in which it participates. The labor union, seashells, and

7

magnetic coils are so thoroughly defined by the incidents in which they take part that their reality might seem identical with the *events* to which they give rise. The objects riding in the wheel seem no better than pawns of their interactions with other things. Some might even call it naive to think of some Buddha-in-itself or electrical coil *an sich* apart from the events in which these objects are involved. In this way the myth suggests that there is no such thing as an "accident" as opposed to substance, and also no such thing as mere "relations" that would be less real than the component pieces of which they are built. The various flags, machines, cats, and foxes in the myth would not be substances undergoing accidental interplay with other objects. They would only be concrete events, deployed in specific relations with all other things.

Nonetheless, the myth also shows the limitations of this philosophy of relations or events. It is certainly true that all of the human and inhuman objects in the myth —those that ride the wheel, live in the underground chambers, or mill around in the streets— are closely linked with the wider series of events in which they are involved. Even so, none of the objects is reducible to the events in which it participates. This becomes clear if we add some additional twists to the story. Along with the banner of the steelworkers' union, we can stipulate that the wheel carries an additional flag— say, a purple lozenge on a field of amber. Once upon a time, this flag would have triggered additional celebration by the union of arrowsmiths. Yet this guild was disbanded long before the wheel was constructed, and therefore never arrived in the underground room reserved for its festival. If the union still existed, the flag would have triggered a memorable event, but this is now destined never to occur. As things stand, the flag is recognized by no one. It is left to circle as a mere piece of fabric or an aesthetic curiosity, with no one aware of its depth of symbolic resonance. Since the flag with the purple lozenge never triggers celebration, some might try to reduce it to its current status amidst the network of things — the state of being viewed with indifference. Yet there is a certain reality possessed by this flag, no matter how cruelly ignored, and someday a new throwback union or sarcastic artist may arise to adopt it as an emblem once more.

Let's simplify the example somewhat, so that only a handful of objects remain in the cars: a plastic cup, a gyroscope, an aircraft engine, and a chunk of plutonium. Now, let's evacuate the underground chambers and fill them with new entities never previously there. What do we learn from such variation? First of all, any living creature in the chambers will be exterminated by the plutonium. But elsewhere, different dramas unfold. There may be an object in one of the chambers that causes the gyroscope to move differently from before. So too, the aircraft engine may be affected in unique ways by some of the entities that have been placed in the various rooms. A few turns of the wheel, and we become bored with these permutations. So let's empty the rooms once more and fill them with hundreds of new objects. Here again we generate a world of new relations that have never previously walked the earth. And no matter how often we are sated with the multitude of combinations between the wheel and the chambers, the supply of novelties is limitless. For as long as there are unlimited funds at our disposal (and this we suppose as a condition of the myth), there are a limitless number of entities that can be placed in the emptied chambers of the trench and the vacant cars of the wheel.

It must be said that there is something to the plutonium, the plastic cup, and the gyroscope that is never exhausted by the various events that occur. New pairings of these objects with other things can always be dreamed up, or even put into effect. And this is where most philosophers would invoke a traditional concept that can only be regarded as misleading: potentiality. For as soon as the specter of potential is raised, the key point has been evaded. It will be said that the various new events involving the plutonium, the plastic cup, and the gyroscope tell us nothing new about the actuality of these objects. Instead, these events only make clear that every object has the *potential* to affect other things in certain ways. On this point the classical and twentieth century theories are in reciprocal agreement. Namely, the classical models invoke potentiality *in order to shut relations out of substance,* since if a single hammer has the potential to build a church, a weapon, or a coffin, it might seem possible to forgive its accidental entanglements in any of these activities while maintaining its private integrity. Conversely, the twentieth century theories invoke potentiality *in order to shut substance out of relations,* since if the hammer is defined by its totality of relations, to speak of its unactualized future states as "potentials" frees us from having to determine where these potentials are located, thereby denying any actuality outside of explicit current relations.

Both the classical and recent theories appeal to "potential" as a disingenuous way of equating the actual with the relational. For if we only say that plutonium has the *potential* to kill whatever creatures enter the underground room, we have betrayed our obligation to decide in what the *actuality* of the plutonium consists. To define a thing as potential is to view it solely from the outside, in terms of the effects it might one day have on other things, and this avoids the question under dispute. For let us consider a variation on the myth in which no living creatures are in the underground chambers at all, with the plutonium circling only past wooden, metallic, and cotton items. Here the lethal character of the plutonium is never triggered, yet this deadliness remains a part of its actuality. The plutonium's act of killing will surely exist only in relation to a living thing, but this misses the point. For I speak here not of the killing (which is obviously a relation) but of that lethal portion of the plutonium's reality that is never manifest in cases where nothing is killed. Even the most ardent philosopher of networks would not deny that there is more to the plutonium than is expressed in any given instant. One will concede that it has an actuality apart from its relations. Yet there is also a disappointing habit of assuming that this extra portion of reality is simply a material substratum supporting many properties not currently expressed. It will be thought that the real action lies on the side of *perception*, of our tortuous and subtle human awareness, which finds ways to add poignant spice to bland slabs of objective material stuff. The high ground of philosophy is given over to a dogmatic brand of materialism, even by those who claim to despise material reality. Against this, I hold that it remains a mystery where and what the actuality of the plutonium really is. It cannot be defined by its current relations, because the reality of the plutonium is precisely what exceeds those relations. What needs to be discovered is an actuality different from all events, but one that belongs to plutonium, armies, flocks of geese, and Hindu epics no less than to atoms.

And this is the possibly misleading point in our myth. As the various passenger objects rise and fall with the motion of the wheel, they trigger a multitude of events. This seems to lead to a twofold ontology in which we have solid physical entities riding in the cars and immaterial events that are triggered by the various interactions. But this is inadequate. For in a sense even the physical objects riding the cars of the wheel are themselves events, since each involves a special configuration of various subcomponents. In order to do justice to the ontology of the world, we must not think of the cats, foxes, or bombs riding the wheel as simple unified lumps. Instead, we must imagine that each of these entities is itself produced by a smaller ferris wheel riding in each car, to represent the interaction of the components of any cat, fox, or bomb. And all of these pieces should be imagined in turn as products of still smaller wheels, these by even tinier wheels, these tinier wheels by minuscule ones, minuscule wheels by micro-wheels, and so on to infinity. Nor does the movement occur only in a downward direction. To complete the myth, we also need to imagine each of the events triggered by our ferris wheel as loaded into a larger wheel in turn. For instance, the celebration of the steelworkers is a potential ingredient in further events, no less than are the flag and workers themselves. As for the crowds milling around in the street, each of them might be considered as made of an inter-locking and infinitely regressing series of ferris wheels, stretching to the depths of Hell and beyond. No point in reality is merely a solid thing, and none is an ultimate concrete event unable to act as a component in further events. In this respect, the cosmos might be described as a vast series of interlocking ferris wheels. Let these trillions of wheels spin in your mind. Let them sink into your heart and enliven your mood. And savor these countless wheels before moving to the myths still to come.

2

The Bridge

In my student years I spent hours wandering by night along the waters near Annapolis. It would be digressive to share my reflections on those morbid strolls amidst tunnels and viaducts, which can be justified only my young age at the time, and by the durable core of insights to which they led. All that was valuable in those long nocturnal walks is closely linked in my mind with the Chesapeake Bay Bridge, a dazzling structure built in 1952 and doubled in size in 1973, the birth year of my youngest brother. (This bridge is mentioned at the outset because of its key role in the myth that follows). While my excessive fondness for the writings of Martin Heidegger ought to have made me despise all human infrastructure as detestable cases of technical stock-piling, my temperament was such that I always *adored* the various towers, cables, steam vents, and slag heaps encountered at various points along my route. And I was regular in that route, rarely deviating each night from the same preordained circuit.

Yet there was another side to life in Annapolis. At the time it would not have been wrong to describe me as a reclusive student of metaphysics from an innocent village in Iowa. Often enough I would decline invitations, retire to my room, and study the works of great thinkers both ancient and modern. But in relaxed periods devoid of stress, another side of my character emerged. Despite visible eccentricities, my jovial *bonhomie* and backslapping ways first made me the favorite of local restaurateurs, and by chain reaction I soon sparkled on the exclusive Annapolis yachting scene. My social stock rose quickly in this world, to the point that I found myself lionized by those jaded scions of the East who had adopted Maryland's capital as their playpen. In the gin-fuelled croquet matches of those years, and in countless lengthy boating trips on Chesapeake Bay, the seeds of my current philosophy were sown. Not that my new friends shared my enthusiasm for the works of Whitehead or Fichte: far from it. But rather than merely tolerating such interests, they treated them as a charming quirk adding luster to the group.

My meteoric rise in this circle of plutocrats eventually peaked in my engagement to Olympia, the multilingual heiress to an ancient pharmaceutical fortune. It pains me to recall that our attachment ended after some months, despite great passion and personal rapport, through the uncomfortable fit of my Protestant background with her Greek Orthodox faith. In a secular age like our own, the claim will sound affected. But it was less a matter of religious difference *per se* than of the incompatible character traits to which our respective creeds gave rise. It is true that Olympia found my eager Midwestern work ethic somewhat repellent; high-society gossip was not far from the mark on this point. But the truly impassible barrier concerned my ardent moralism in matters of public policy. The point is best illustrated by a remarkable passage of de Tocqueville on the subject of crime:

> In Europe, the criminal is an unfortunate who is fighting to save his head from agents of the government. The people are merely onlookers in this contest. In America, he is an enemy of the human race and has all humanity against him ...

> During my stay in the United States, I saw the inhabitants of one county in which a major crime had been committed

spontaneously organize committees to apprehend the guilty party and turn him over to the courts.[1]

In this respect (though in few others) I was the stereotypical product of my nation. Reports of crime stirred a white-hot rage in my heart, with an intensity that placed great burdens on my more placid fiancée. And though my diligent studies and ample social life left no time to organize actual committees for pursuit of criminals, I wasted much energy in swearing that I would do so. At a distance of many years, it is easy to recognize the callous immaturity of my behavior; if Olympia is now beyond all retrieval and even all contact, the fault is entirely my own.

But the topic here is philosophy, and in this field Olympia was my superior in both talent and instinct. Despite her Greek heritage, she scorned the great works of the schools of Athens. As an adolescent she was drawn to the assertive transitional era of Bruno, Bacon, and Hobbes; when the Deleuzian fashion finally appeared, she was carried away quickly by that current. Yet she soon displayed a preference for the closely allied works of Gilbert Simondon, whose critique of hylemorphism became the pillar of her philosophy. Though never a confessed monist, she dismissed with impatience my liking for what she called "fully-formed individuals." While I remained committed to specific objects, Olympia championed a vague notion of "pre-objects." Our debates on this point were always respectful, unlike our running dispute on the origins of crime, which then — if not now — I ascribed to inherent taint in the criminal soul.

One day we sat on a bench at the edge of the bay, exchanging honorific poems: not about each other (we both viewed the practice as passé) but on themes raised in Plato's *Parmenides*. Olympia's brilliant sonnet was written in honor of the One, while my equally skilled work was devoted to praise of the Many. In response to my poem, Olympia deployed a half-hour polemic against the weakness of my position. The tension of our dispute led her to such daring formulations that I briefly wondered if she was right. As I stared across the waters at the Chesapeake Bay Bridge, she reminded me that she was born and raised just a stone's throw from the structure. But while I respected her childhood fondness for the bridge, I ignored her nostalgic comments this time; my thoughts were elsewhere. Though I do not feel at liberty to reproduce Olympia's speech in this book (she may one day reappear), it is obviously my right to retell the myth that occurred to me then.

"We sit not far from the monument of your childhood, close enough to see human figures walking along the bridge. They seem not to move with clear purpose in one direction, as they would if departing a damaged vehicle for help. Instead they hesitate, or even move in reverse. With no obvious reason for their behaving this way, we are permitted to speculate freely on their motives. Though thinkers and artists might stroll at random for numerous reasons, such people are few in number even in cities as cultured as Annapolis. Hence it is likely that these are cases of emotional disturbance. And we might well conclude that these people intend the bridge as a platform for the destruction of inanimate things. For there is inherent fascination in watching everyday objects drop from a great height— all the more so if these items vanish magically into the sea. As a thought experiment, we take this to be the purpose of the human figures seen hazily on the bridge: we assume that they jettison various entities over the railing and watch them tumble into the bay. Although we might imagine that they simply toss over the railings those random objects that are close at hand, it is more likely that each is specially fascinated with one particular class of entity for sacrifice to Poseidon. For some it would be only glassy objects. For others it might be jewels, assuming these could be obtained in sufficient quantity. Statuettes of historical figures might be the favorite of another type of vagrant, while others would show more outlandish tastes: refusing to launch any item not having octagonal shape, or not covered with glitter. Perhaps a number of truck drivers catch the disease as well, and risk their careers by abandoning cargoes to these madmen for the mere sake of spectacle. The entire scenario is improbable, I will admit. But so is most political philosophy and the whole of mathematics.

"My Olympia, this image may seem only obliquely related to our disagreement. But you know me well, and can guess the trend of my thinking. Each object plunges from the bridge into the cold waters of the bay, which you know to be sufficiently dirtied that the object is lost from sight once it enters the water. Even the striped bass and needlefish that inhabit the bay cannot be seen from above. For all we know from direct experience, free of inference, the waters of the Chesapeake may as well be a single pre-Socratic mass. It is not the water of Thales (for there is more than water in this polluted mixture) but the *apeiron* of Anaximander and his rivals: a boundless plenum in which all things are one. If we consider a limit case in which all objects in the universe were jettisoned from the Chesapeake Bay Bridge, the fantasy fails only for contingent practical reasons: namely, we admit that the bay has a finite depth. Rather than being dissolved in the waters, most objects endure beneath the sea as long as they do not rust or rot, and this may take hundreds of years. In principle a salvage company could even be hired to retrieve some of the lost items. In short, it is only for us and not in themselves that the objects expelled from the bridge will vanish from the cosmos. Hence the destruction of entities by tossing them from the Bay Bridge is not only implausible in practical terms, but in metaphysical terms quite impossible.

For this reason we shift to a more nightmarish setting than the Chesapeake Bay. You, Olympia, have long admired the images of Hell proposed by the religions of the world..."

Here she flinched slightly, since this was a false and needless jab on my part. Olympia had never shared my enthusiasm even for Dante, let alone my disreputable taste for fantasy paintings of the underworld. I collected such pictures with relish, and wryly hung them over shelves assembling the volumes of Tertullian with those of my puritanical countryman, the ghastly Jonathan Edwards. This literary and pictorial fascination with the tortures of the damned (which I never took for religious truth) had been another of many points of tension between us. But I ignored her reaction, and continued the story with vigor.

"In your honor, then, we shift the scene to the depths of Hell itself. Imagine an exact replica of the Chesapeake Bay Bridge, spanning a lake of molten lead in one of the lower infernal regions. Rather than mere disturbed vagrants, we now have actual devils dropping objects into liquefied metal. Suppose they are the demons of *Inferno* XXI. You will recall the irony, for historians of seventeenth century philosophy, that those demons belong to the so-called 'Malebranche' tribe. You know their names by heart: the chief Malacoda and his minions Alichino, Calcabrina, Cagnazzo, Barbariccia, Libicocco, Draghignazzo, Ciriatto, Graffiacane, Farfarello, and Rubicante. They are names befitting an evil troupe of Italian players, but with hurtful weapons rather than slapsticks and wooden syringes. These demons of the Malebranche kick glass and plastic objects from the bridge and watch them plummet into the searing lake, never to regain individual form. Rumors spread through Hell of impending annihilation for all individual things. As a known champion of objects, I am summoned by Virgil to cross the Styx and defend the various chairs, horses, pine trees, hammers, and stones that the demons push into that molten lake where all is one. En route to our conflict with these howling fiends, we pass through Limbo to visit the horde of pre-Socratic thinkers, recruiting them for our journey into darkness.

"Upon arrival at the bridge, we are terrified and enraged to witness a legion of objects dropping to destruction in the lead. Among them are countless beautiful items, as well as living creatures whose wails of despair while falling cause Virgil, Pythagoras, and I to cover our ears in pity. After several hours of oaths and weeping, our party regains its composure and approaches the functionaries of Hell at the foot of the bridge near the smoking lake of lead. The demons descend rapidly from the bridge, surrounding us with their tridents and spears, and jabber that we are next to be pushed into the lake. 'Silence!,' Virgil cries, followed by words carefully arranged in a form resembling *terza rima*:

These figures who you see here cloaked in shadow,
they are not men, but once were men of Hellas:
Milesians or of Elea, now in Limbo.

Their souls had crossed the river unredeemed,
before the great Redeemer washed our souls.
Devoid of Grace, their *physis* was their idol.

This one by my side who is no shadow,
he is no Hellene, but an Iowan;
instead of Nature, objects are his love.

Oh, wretched demons! Do not block my mission,
for I am sent by He who wakes the dead:
the Second Person of the Triune One.

Our Lord in Heaven wishes us a struggle
with words, and not your rusty forks and tongs,
on whether things are many, things are one.

But if we fail, then fairness will allow
that each who fails abandons claim to soul,
and in the lead shall melt into the One.

Shifting into prose, Virgil then makes detailed arrangements with the demons for the conditions of our duel. Whoever refutes the claim that the molten lake is the ground of all things shall depart the underworld intact, liberated along with all the previously doomed objects, hauled and escorted back to the sun by an honor guard of centaurs and basilisks. But all who fail shall be pushed to oblivion in the lake.

"The pre-Socratics have inspected the scene carefully, and conclude that the demons have infinite time and power at their disposal. Thus it seems clear that if things continue as they have, all objects in the cosmos are fated to vanish in the molten lead. This being the case, these early Greeks would each try to claim that the lake justifies his own theory rather than those of his rivals. The first to step forward are Thales defender of water, and Anaximenes king of air. Both concede that while they may have been wrong about the nature of ultimate substance, it is a small step from water or air to calling *lead* the first principle of everything. This obvious sophistry is rejected by the demons without comment, and the two great Ionian thinkers are dispatched via pitchfork into the molten sea. Empedocles comes next, but has abandoned all hope in advance. Given that his two great forerunners failed to prove the analogy between molten lead and even *one* physical element, Empedocles sees that his fourfold system of air, earth, fire, and water stands no chance of success in explaining the infernal lake. Having already plunged into the crater of Mt. Aetna to destroy his earthly body, this prophet-like figure now earns a hero's death, discarding his very soul with a similar leap.

"Heraclitus the Obscure, that dark knight of flux and fire, now feels on the verge of triumph. He explains his theories with pompous declamations as if victory were foreordained. Yet he is struck dumb when the demons note that there is no flux of becoming in the lead at all, which remains nondescript and motionless. Too startled even to protest, he is shoved into the lake, his soul beyond retrieval even by the merciful Trinity. Democritus rises next in defense of his theory. He would make the more plausible case that even lead is not purely homogeneous, but made of smaller component atoms. There is no refuting this claim, and hence the infernal hordes of the Malebranche huddle in conspiracy, plotting a way to cheat Democritus of his soul. After some minutes the demon Malacoda emerges from the group and emits a sickly whistling sound. Upon this signal, a deformed bat with three fetal heads and a cobra for a tail flaps obscenely from its hook beneath the bridge— spittle dripping from malformed mouths as it asks the wish of its master in what sounds like a creolized dialect of Sumerian. And now Malacoda lets out four or five more whistles both quavering and shrill. The bat chuckles hideously and steers away rapidly. Its flight is too quick to follow its course toward Satan, locked in the icy crust at the center of the planet, chewing slowly on the bloodied husks of Brutus, Cassius, and Judas. Two minutes later we guess that the bat has addressed the Prince of Darkness in person, for the lead begins to recede. But soon it is replaced by inscrutable material resembling the primal stuff of the dawn of the cosmos. Even the untrained observer would note its more shapeless character than the quark-gluon plasma of the supposed inflationary phase of the universe. The demons welcome this new lake of featureless material, with its nearly infinite temperature and density. Into these waterless waters they drive the unlucky and wailing soul of Democritus.

"The trend of the exercise now becomes clear. What the demons always intended was to winnow the field to advocates of the *apeiron*, that formless and boundless being that provided the chief pre-Socratic alternative to the supremacy of water, air, or atoms. Not that the demons wish this group well, either: they simply find them more of an interesting challenge. The great Anaximander is the first to approach the newly shapeless, primeval lake, whose baffling pre-liquid straddles the border of nonentity. Somewhat disheartened, he observes that justice demands that the *apeiron* arise at the end of time, millions of years in the future, closely resembling the conditions of this very lake. Hence there is no need to enter the lead at this stage: a mere forcing of the inevitable. Malacoda chimes bitterly that the road to a million years begins with a single step, and poor Anaximander is tripped and toppled into the lake that knows no form.

"Next comes Parmenides. With the skill of a lawyer, he artfully claims that dropping objects into the lake is a vulgar and needless solution, since the diverse entities of experience are already illusions; being already is, and all else is not. Malacoda responds with a shrieking rejoinder: 'Then it makes no difference where you stand!' He deals the death blow once more, with a swift kick to the grandfatherly Eleatic master. After a similar exchange, Xenophanes is pushed to his doom. That leaves Pythagoras and Anaxagoras, the two advocates of an ancient *apeiron* that was later split into pieces— for the former through inhaling void, for the latter through rapid spinning and vibration by the workings of a powerful Mind. But Rubicante, most learned of the demons, informs his chief coldly that Pythagoras works at cross purposes, since he also made *number* the substance of all. No further excuse is needed. The demons drag the geometer to the edge of the lake. They add a final insulting touch by scrawling numbers on his cloak, both integers and his hated irrationals, before pushing his soul into the void.

"The trial of Anaxagoras is a lengthier saga. Like you, Olympia, I hold him to be the greatest of the pre-Socratics. As is well known, the *apeiron* in his theory rotated so rapidly through the power of Mind that it broke into pieces, which Aristotle termed the *homoiomereiai*." I was now beginning to sound like the mentor addressing the teenaged girl in *Sophie's World*, a potentially grievous insult for a natural genius like Olympia.[2] But her temperament was always modest, and she looked unperturbed. And so I continued in the same vein.

"For Anaxagoras, since all that exists arose from the same monolithic block of reality, everything contains pieces of everything else. Even in my body there are pieces of horse, shark, tiger, and tree, though the pieces *of me* are dominant and hence I appear as what I am, rather than as these other things. The point of the theory is twofold. First, it provides an explanation of how one thing transforms into another: if I am devoured by sharks and my flesh converted into their own, this is clarified through the fact that I am already somewhat shark-like. Second, it tries to show that things can appear as distinct despite their common root in a unified whole. But you know I hold this idea to be false.

"Your theory is like many others of our Deleuzian era in roughly following the basic principles of Anaxagoras. That is to say, you do not claim that the world is simply a united whole, as the full-blown thinkers of shapeless *apeiron* do. Rather, you contend that the world is both one and many at the same time. Any given object is already interwoven with all others in a sort of continuum. Whatever happens in the world does not result from contact between one individual entity and another, but happens at the level of a united *apeiron*, though you hedge your bets by calling it both hetero-geneous and continuous. Since I am not fully myself, and the shark and tree also not fully themselves, we are all laced with difference. No causal relation exists at the level of individual things; such individuals are not really cut off from each other in the first place. But the pernicious consequence is that the same thing will be simultaneously 'a battleship, a wall, and a human being,' in Aristotle's memorable phrase.[3]

"Now Olympia, you always respond that the various individual things are not just 'potentially' distinct, but 'virtually' so. Yet here is the problem. Either the various beings dissolved in the lake of lead remain distinct, or they do not. If not then we have monism, and there is no reason that different entities would ever emerge from it. But if they do remain distinct, then there is the rather different problem of knowing why they are more than merely one. For how is the virtual *shark* different from the virtual *tree*? You want them to be a continuum, but this is a step that Aristotle knew could not be taken. Remember your *Physics*, for you have studied it closely. In that work Aristotle treats time, change, and number as continua in which different individuals are only potentially present rather than actually so. But recall that he never says the same about substance itself. Although a given university classroom can be mentally divided into three, seven, fifty, or ten thousand physical sectors according to mood, it is not the case that the number of *students* in the room is potentially three, seven, fifty, or ten thousand. There is always a certain actual number of students, whatever that number may be. Hence I deny your claim that actual objects are the surface result of a deeper continuum of pre-individuals enveloped in a virtual state. There is no way to avoid some concept of individual substance, and hence Anaxagoras is guilty like the rest. More in sadness than in anger, I leave him to the demons and their relentless punishment. I need not describe what they did, but be aware that the great Anaxagoras is no more. Who shall wash the blood from my hands? For when I turned for consolation to the Mantuan poet, he was gone. Where was Virgil? Virgil had gone."

The myth having concluded, I hoped for one of Olympia's warm rejoinders, which usually took the form of a counterexample striking at the root of some overlooked prejudice. But for the first and last time I was disappointed. Olympia responded, a bit pretentiously for such a down-to-earth woman, in French. Her words were those of Simondon: "L'opération technique qui impose une forme à une matière passive et indéterminée... c'est essentiellement l'opération commandée par l'homme libre et exécutée par l'esclave..."[4] The tone was gracious and healing. But the content was appalling, for it ventured direct analogy between my theory and the dictates of a master to a passively obedient slave. And this from someone who had never shown the least sympathy for postcolonial currents. There was the aggravating factor that my system has never contained any passive or indeterminate matter in the first place, or any matter at all, but only an infinite regress of *forms*. Later she apologized for the remark, which she blamed on her annoyance over my lengthy discussion of Hell, a place whose existence she denied even more adamantly than I did. And all was set right again.

A few days later we had another of our recurrent arguments: as usual, it concerned the rehabilitation of offenders under an imagined perfect state. The final bell had tolled, and our engagement —that glorious era!— came to a close. The Myth of the Bay Bridge was the final discussion of significance that we ever held. But since love remains always in peril, while philosophy is forever, I will confess that the memory is more sweet than bitter.

3

Tiny Calliopes

The 2007-08 academic year was my first period of sabbatical from the American University in Cairo. Invited warmly to join the faculty in Amsterdam, I spent a semester there lecturing on metaphysics and the philosophy of science, not far from the canals, the museums, and the vices of that magical city. By springtime I had left the Netherlands on my third trip to the subcontinent of India, based this time in the state of Tamil Nadu. Arriving at Chennai Airport in the dead of night, I hailed an autorickshaw and made my way to a dusty hotel on Triplicane High Road. There, a more than bearable lifestyle soon took shape: long walks for iced drinks during the sweltering afternoons, televised cricket matches by night in the company of *papadum* and Kingfisher beer.

On this trip two distinct sides of my personality struggled for dominance. In one respect I had never been in a more scientific and sceptical frame of mind. Under the influence of acquaintances, I had become a zealous (though temporary) devotee of the living German thinker Thomas Metzinger, who reduces all problems of philosophy to questions of the brain. His *Being No One*,[5] that remorseless *opus magnum*, now emboldened me to scoff at the assorted ghosts, fairies, and unicorns that filled the philosophies of the unlearned, with their fear of scientific rigor. At times this new standpoint even awoke a spirit of physical assertion: though it was highly out of character, I remember once feeling the wish to shove several priests as they passed me on a sidewalk in Chennai. Though I would never have acted on this disgraceful impulse, I have since repented with liberal gifts to the poor.

But after several days of adjusting to the surroundings of Chennai, my familiar self returned. This self has always respected the mystic pieties of those more schooled than I in the various Holy Scriptures of the world. With my birthday approaching, I was concerned at the time with the notion of *fate*. Advancing age increased my uncertainty as to whether one's life is shaped by lucky contingencies, or whether numerous different chances generally lead the same human character to the same basic outcome. Deeply perplexed by the matter, I scheduled a meeting in Chennai's remotest neighborhood with an expatriate *québécoise* astrologer. This erudite middle-aged woman offered mixed signals of my destiny. As I had painfully known for years, the moon at my birth was afflicted, portending long years of ostracism and gloom. For while the moon is stationed in charming and light-hearted Libra, it breaches the cusp of the shadowy twelfth house, where it stands in crippling opposition to weighty Saturn in the sixth. This latter factor heralded not only sadness, but possible confinement through mental illness. There was the further aggravating factor, known to me but withheld from Madame Laval, that this strife of moon and Saturn was inherited equally from *both* of my parents, suggesting a familial legacy of sorrow. Nonetheless, other factors at my birth provided an almost comical refutation of these evil omens, and promised a life of successful audacity and outrageous good luck. The Part of Fortune, taken most seriously by the Arabs of Mesopotamia, was placed in my chart in the expansive fifth house, conjunct the cardinal point of Aries. Meanwhile, the supposedly afflicted Saturn made a perfect trine with Jupiter in Leo in the tenth, foretelling remarkable benefits in career matters with little to no effort on my part, especially toward middle age. The somber ringed planet also formed an exact biquintile with Neptune in the first, suggesting the power of giving rigorous structure to all that would otherwise be strange. And finally, the three outer planets —and *only* these three— were found in retrograde motion. By the teachings of C.G. Jung, this signaled my innate mastery of a large stock of unconscious archetypes.

Departing in confusion over these ambivalent messages, I faced the future with apprehension, unaware that an evening of hilarious bonuses lay in store. First, I opened my email account and found news of a small inheritance from a distant relative. Second, the hotel clerk moved me into a corner suite as a personal favor; the new room offered an excellent view of the lively Triplicane High Road. Third, I took dinner at a nondescript restaurant where waiters served an outstanding *dosa*, their excellent manners making me feel like visiting royalty. Fourth, I entered an unpromising used bookstore and was shocked to discover a pristine first edition of Alexius Meinong's masterpiece *Über Annahmen*, a formidable precursor of my own object-oriented philosophy. And fifth, lucky timing enabled me to capitalize on a brief but dramatic fluctuation in exchange rates. As was sometimes the case when departing Cairo on travel abroad, I had failed to obtain the mainstream hard currencies, and had settled instead for a bundle of Saudi riyals. Through geopolitical quirks not worth recalling, the riyal surged that evening against the Indian rupee for a period of some ninety minutes, during which time I happened to approach the exchange window. Thanks to this windfall, the remainder of my trip would assume an unexpected air of luxury.

Pleased with my good fortune, I made the quarter-hour walk to Marina Beach, briefly saddened by memories of those who had perished there in the great tsunami. As I sat alone on a cement pillar, looking off into the deadly Bay of Bengal, my initial thoughts concerned the evening's lucky events. But soon my mind returned to the Leibnizian doctrine of "tiny animals," those minuscule bodies from which no monad is ever free, whether before birth or after death. As will soon appear, I had several objections to this unusual theory. But at once I was startled from my reverie by a solitary Tamil child who marched past banging on a snare drum. The relative slowness of his motion meant that I listened to his drumming for three or four minutes before it faded away to the north. Barely had the child vanished before a group of cricket fans came up the beach, bravely waving the banner not of the local Super Kings, but of a rival franchise. They shook black tambourines and followed the same route as the child with the drum, and their rattling procession faded at precisely the same rate. Next came the low point in this train of musicians: a slovenly tuba player belting out pompous arias in a key that might be called "minor" if it had shown any coherence at all. Luckily this player also marched away to the north, and soon his music was no more. It now felt as though I were observing a picturesque and slow-motion parade, organized by some deviant mastermind of the third-world *biennali*. No sooner had I formed this thought than a family of Hindu acrobats came striding into view, clad in sparkling costume and the regional variant of the jester's cap, while singing carnivalesque anthems I had heard somewhere before— presumably in Slovakia during my disastrous tour of circuses there. The acrobats gradually disappeared to the north at the predictable rate to which I was now accustomed. But the next musical act that came up the beach did not disappear to the north, or anywhere else. It appeared instead on the southern edge of the beach, moved toward me at the usual slothful rate, but then parked by my side and remained there for hours to come. Surely it must have been manned, yet I no longer recall anything but the machine itself. This, then, was the culmination of my lucky evening: a battered steam calliope, just barely out of tune, playing complex fugues in both the Western and Indian styles. It made me think once more of Leibniz.

The calliope first appeared in the mid-nineteenth century under a patent granted to one Joshua C. Stoddard of Massachusetts; its fortunes rose and fell with those of steam engines more generally. Though it failed comically in its early purpose to replace church bells, it soon found a more plausible home on riverboats, and even more so in the circus. There it served as the harmless accompanist to flame-eaters and mimes, and to this day calliope albums are normally classed as children's music. But if the masks and cosmetics, the skilled tricks and exotic animals of the circus permit the calliope to serve as an innocent backdrop, its unnatural qualities have given it the reverse aspect of horror as well. It is widely known that Pierrot, Harlequin, and the other clowns of the *commedia dell'arte* became special pets of the absinthe-swilling *Décadents* of Montmartre, and of Schoenberg's grotesque quintet. The theme of circus clowns as purveyors of murder is such a well-worn feature of American popular culture that the costume is now worn even by killers of no education and little intelligence. The calliope itself has not escaped this general trend. Employed by such figures as Hitchcock to provide a droll atmosphere for terrible crimes, and hauled through today's Europe by the seediest crews, the innocent calliope has gradually become suspect in its motives. Rarely in perfect tune even when fresh from the factory, its increasing misfires with age nudge it by degrees toward outright atonality. I was not surprised that the engine now parked next to me on the Chennai beach was well past its harmonic prime. Nor was I shocked to find it covered with dust and grit, in a manner suggesting Kafka's armored insect.

Despite the known maxim that "everything is connected," the things of this world are remarkably separate from one another, often with little connection beyond conjunctions produced by the mind. The chances of anyone ever mentioning a calliope in the same breath as Leibniz were always somewhat limited. But this musical instrument happened to park by my side at the very moment when I reflected deeply on his metaphysics of monads; in this way, a monstrous blind date was arranged between the rusted calliope and Leibniz's theory of "tiny animals." The metaphysics of Leibniz is presented most vividly in the pair of brief masterworks composed in old age at Vienna in 1714: *Principles of Nature and Grace*, and the more famous *Monadology*. The part of his metaphysics relevant here is the claim that the monad (simple substance) is never separated from its body (composite substance). The rule has but one exception: "there are also no completely separated souls, nor spirits without bodies. *God alone* is completely detached from bodies."[6] Otherwise, monad and body are always found together: "There are simple substances everywhere ... and each distinct simple substance or monad, which makes up the center of a composite substance (an animal, for example) and is the principle of its unity, is surrounded by a *mass* composed of an infinity of other monads, which constitute the *body belonging to* this central monad ..."[7] And finally, "Each monad, together with a particular body makes up a living substance. Thus, there is not only life everywhere, joined to the limbs or organs, but there are also infinite degrees of life in the monads, some dominating more or less over others."[8]

For years Leibniz had been the thinker dearest to my heart. But I also saw a number of flaws in his theory in need of some remedy. While I adored his model of isolated individual substance, he also proclaimed several views that I detested, all of them linked in some way to his theory of monad and body. Unlike most of my friends, I held passionately that simple substances must lie behind all composites. Over the years it had become fashionable to say that everything is constituted of relations. Yet the fact remained that a thing cannot be entirely formed of its current relations, or it would never have any reason to change; there would be no surplus behind its current state of affairs that would promote the emergence of anything new. Heidegger's theory of tools had proven that the hammer is irreducible to its effects on any wider system of things, as shown by the surprising breakdowns that disrupt its current system of involvements. While realism remained out of fashion, for me it became ironclad law. Nonetheless, I could not accept all the conclusions that Leibniz drew from the undeniable *simplicity* of his monads.

On the positive side, two aspects of the Leibnizian philosophy entered most deeply into my dreams. The first was the principle that monads have no windows. Whatever Leibniz's reputation for personal cheerfulness, his vision of trillions of entities cut off one from one another, each lodged in a private vacuum accessible only to God, could inspire nothing but horror. Yet that horror was of a salutary kind, and formed the bedrock of my personal view of the cosmos. Not that I agreed with Leibniz that the pre-established harmony of things by God was a feasible solution: quite the contrary, despite my openness to religion when compared with my atheistic peers. Rather, what I liked about this appeal to divine intervention was its air of great seriousness concerning the depth of the problem, which appeared so insoluble that routing all relations through God seemed wonderfully frank in its desperation. Barring adoption of Leibniz's optimistic theology, the unified monads are left to recede into permanent darkness. For many reasons I found this picture attractive. The second aspect of Leibniz that moved me to reflection was the dualism between the unity of monads and their plurality of features. Against British Empiricism and its frivolous "bundles of qualities" —a merely critical notion in which the bundling action is left as obscure as in the most evasive theologies— I agreed that the realities in the world must be units. Yet these units also demanded a plurality of traits if they were not to become mutually interchangeable, with palm trees equipped to perform the labor of volcanoes and vice versa.

Yet there were also two principles of Leibniz that I found especially dangerous. One was his assumption that along with being *unified*, the monad must also be *simple*. His monad was granted no parts, and its multitude of qualities stemmed not from these forbidden pieces, but from *relations* placed miraculously in its heart by the Deity. This led him to a false distinction between ultimate, simple substances and complex, derivative aggregates. The calliope now raging by my side was not allowed genuine reality by Leibniz any more than a ring of candles or brigade of mercenaries would be. But simply from observing and hearing the musical engine, I knew this claim to be false. The calliope's sweet-and-sour melodies shifted constantly from one instant to the next. Always slightly out of key, the instrument edged between Indian scales and a vaguely Western musical scheme. At times I felt restored to the age of the *Upanishads*, and at others to a Baroque court in Austria. Sad music played at one moment, exuberant hymns in the next. In the end the calliope even slipped into an especially twisted rendering of the tritely imperialistic "Colonel Bogey," with wild arpeggiated trills that only an intelligent agent could design. Indeed, the instrument changed its tune so constantly that one could never identify that invincible machine with what it played at any moment, any continuous stretch of ten seconds, or even with the sum total of music I had heard during the entire evening. The Empiricists were misled to hold that we encounter individual qualities and then link them together through the gullible myth of an underlying thing. Instead,

Husserl and his heirs were more on the mark in saying that we first confront the calliope as a whole, so that the eerie underlying style of the object imbues all of the isolated songs and notes that emanate from it.

Persisting through all its varying sounds, the calliope was an enduring unit by comparison with the changing sensual qualities it emitted moment by moment. Yet neither was it simple in the downward direction, as we move toward its pieces. Only a fool would call the calliope a simple atom without parts, since the most cursory glance showed it to have numerous whistles, valves, and a small inner fireplace of brick or iron (I could hardly see which in the darkness). Yet from this multitude of parts, a single musical engine emerged. Just as the calliope was independent of the specific notes it played at each moment, and separate as well from its shifting effects on me and the sixty or seventy other listeners on the beach, so too it achieved an autonomous life over and above its component pieces. Never could the calliope be dismissed as a mere aggregate, since most of its pieces could be removed, replaced, shuffled, or altered without the calliope ceasing to be what it was. In short, the Leibnizian difference between substance and aggregate was shown to be false. The calliope was no less unified than the simplest hydrogen atom, yet this fact did not entail an absence of tinier components. Everything in the cosmos was both substance and aggregate. Reductionism was false; geology, sociology, and rhetoric need not bow before the anger and arrogance of smug eliminators.

Next to me the calliope continued piping its shrill tunes, remaining the same while emitting qualities that linked with my moods to form new resolutions and new realities. And I saw that this was equally true of each valve and whistle, which remained the same despite their multitude of effects on the outer world, and despite the myriad molecules of which they were composed. Each of these pieces could be imagined as a strange calliope in its own right, even if the music was subtler or more banal for mere copper valves than for the instrument as a whole. Like the calliope, every entity remained itself in two directions, reducible neither upward nor downward: not reducible to an "event" as with the ferris wheel, but also not to a searing lake of sub-plasma near the basin of Hell. Each speck of being now seemed like a terrible instrument disgorging its music upward, but born only as the result of equally terrible songs emitted from its pieces below. Much as with the interlocking ferris wheels of the first chapter, I now saw that the world could be conceived as a series of interlocking calliopes, each emitting music into the local sky above it, and thereby combining with others to yield larger machines. This sense was heightened further by the shrill quarter-tones of the calliope as it unleashed a wild march at the fastest tempo I had ever heard. A terrible moment was almost at hand. But before this happened, I grasped in a flash the thin line dividing Leibnizian doctrine from Heidegger's obscure praise of the fourfold structure of things. At the deepest layer of the real, Leibniz envisioned a strife between unified monads and their plurality of features. Above that deepest layer, all was sheer aggregate: clocks, forests, and armies were merely "things of reason" rather than genuine entities. By simply removing the needless barrier between simple and composite, by realizing that all things are both at once, the duel of the entity with its qualities was doubled. Before me was the phantasmal calliope, unleashing its music into the night while retaining some sort of identity. Yet this instrument as I saw it was merely a phantasm of the real calliope itself, deeper than any perception of it. Within my experience the calliope was in strife with its qualities for me, yet the same strife occurred in depths no experience could reach.

And now came that terrible moment that swept away the previous good fortune of the evening. Among my numerous psychological quirks was a fear related to death: not the expected terror of death *per se*, but an obsessive worry that I might have born with an innate memory of my final moments on earth. What I feared was not sudden and invincible extinction, but certain minor images or careless remarks that would trigger my inborn memories of the moments *preceding* death— so that I would spend my final moments on earth knowing the close was approaching, with each tiny incident a trauma as I stepped toward the end times. But the horror now launched by the calliope was much worse than this. For the instrument suddenly unleashed a terrible variation on one of the least distinguished fugues of Bach, and in this way it triggered innate recollection not of my own final moments, but of the final few years of the cosmos as a whole. I suddenly felt that I had seen the end times before my birth, with this terrible driving tune as the first instant of the world's decline. The beetle-like calliope, I now thought I remembered, would recall the tsunami to India. It would draw leaping flares from the surface of the sun. It would subtly degrade the orbit of the moon to a lower shell, thereby corrupting and augmenting the tides. And with these memories I recoiled all the more to remember my new theory that all entities were larger and smaller calliopes just like this one: trillions of calliopes, reaching down to infinite depths.

4

Offshore Drilling Rig

With an air of impatience, China Miéville recited yet another passage of Lovecraft from memory, almost without error: "At bottom of torso rough but dissimilarly functioning counterparts of head arrangements exist. Bulbous light-grey pseudoneck, without gill suggestions, holds greenish five-pointed starfish-arrangement. Tough, muscular arms 4 feet long and tapering from 7 inches diameter at base to 2.5 at point. To each point is attached small end of a greenish five-veined membraneous triangle 8 inches long and 6 wide at farther end."[9] His errors in recollecting the passage were so trivial that I noticed them only weeks later, when consulting Houellebecq's citation of the text.[10] China had made a few minor slips with the numbers; otherwise, it was a flawless performance.

But even if I had recognized those petty stumbles at the time, I would have held my tongue, for the tone of our conversation had intensified too rapidly in recent hours. Through a series of unforeseen events, we found ourselves stranded without assistance on an offshore oil rig in the Gulf of Mexico, with the early stages of a hurricane nearly upon us. China is widely celebrated as a novelist of the Steampunk current, and to a smaller number of readers is known as an astute Marxist theorist of international law.[11] Recently I had learned that he sought to combine these two genres in a planned masterwork with the provisional title *Crisis Energy*. As we spoke one day during a symposium break at Goldsmiths College, University of London, China mentioned in passing his plan to visit a series of remote oil-drilling facilities in pursuit of atmospheric inspiration for his coming book. He had long been aware of my own fascination with degenerate industrial plants, and when I remarked that our mutual friend Michelle Speidel was now employed in the oil services industry, a simple phone call sufficed to set our plans in motion. In three to four days, Michelle and her colleagues had arranged the entire trip on our behalf.

China began the journey from Providence, and I from Damascus. Both of us traveled without incident to the chosen meeting place: a flood-battered outpost in the miasmic backwaters of rural Louisiana. A heliport used by the petroleum industry was located not far from the place, and after some difficulty we were able to hitch a ride in a passing Hummer, a gluttonous vehicle made even more sinister by its smoked-glass windows. We arrived at the landing pad to find that our timing was perfect: the very helicopter on which we were scheduled was set to depart, its blades already whirring. Alone on the two-hour ride to the offshore platform, we spoke mostly of Egypt, where China had spent some time as a teacher in the Delta city of al-Mansura. Our shared interest in the country made the time pass quickly, and we were not yet bored upon reaching the rig that Michelle's contacts had selected for our tour. It was a textbook example of a tension-leg platform, in the storied Magnolia field at the edge of the so-called Titan Mini-Basin. Here, I reflected, oilmen expelled their souls through tubes toward the core of the earth, siphoning the remains of ancient ferns and reptiles in return. But since we had not come to this offshore field for industrial reasons, let alone political ones, neither China nor I had read up on the details of the process.

We were greeted at the platform by a manager and two workers: a small number of employees, it seemed to me. The first item of business was a tour of the facilities. The worker who guided us, a blunt but sensitive gentleman with the unlikely name of Jonas, had sufficient literary sensibility to gloss over the technical aspects of the offshore setting. He focused instead on the more picturesque aspects of the scene. Foremost among these was the northward vista, where a dozen or more other platforms covered the horizon. Though we knew them all to be in perfect working order, the varying degrees of shadow in which they were displayed made each appear in a different state of advanced decrepitude, like the ruins of a future oceanic civilization devised by Albert Speer. Initially Jonas was to remain with us while the helicopter took the two others on an inspection visit to a platform just out of view. But for reasons no longer remembered, he decided to join the inspection trip, joking that China and I would find more inspiration from being left with an illusion of abandonment, and reassuring us that they would be gone for at most two hours. Having no objection to the plan, we bade them farewell, whereupon we found ourselves the sole occupants of the platform.

Shortly after their departure, the weather darkened. We thought nothing of it, assuming that the industry must have firm procedures to monitor storms and evacuate all personnel with ample margin for safety. Yet we did start to worry as the promised two-hour absence stretched toward six and then seven hours. Some weeks later we learned by chance that the helicopter had gone down just out of view, killing all aboard. At the time, however, it seemed that worsening weather conditions were the most likely reason for our being left alone on the rig. The alert Jonas had taken my cellular telephone number, and should have been able to reach me (were he not already dead). But soon after his departure I had foolishly played a toss-and-catch game with the phone over a padded surface on the platform, during which I had clumsily knocked it into the Gulf. Enraged by the incident, I cursed myself for this lack of dexterity. China

downplayed my worries and reached for his own telephone—
but cursed just as loudly after finding that he had left it
behind in the Hummer, which somewhere insulted the purity
of the mainland. As our worries increased, we began to
examine the communication equipment in the platform's
office, but found it too complicated for our own use.

Approximately seventeen hours after our arrival, there
was still no sign of our guides. Food and water were plentiful,
but the weather had now become dangerous, and a glance at
our watches showed that it was two o'clock in the morning.
Under these risky conditions we had both become somewhat
irritable, and there began a mild argument over our
respective jacket blurbs for Reza Negarestani's controversial
book, the *Cyclonopedia*.[12] I was able to quote China's blurb
sarcastically from memory: "Incomparable. Post-genre
horror, apocalypse theology and the philosophy of oil,
crossbred into a new and necessary codex." Though I agreed
with almost all of his words, including "incomparable," I
found myself in the mood for pedantic objections to the
phrase "new and necessary." It was difficult to refuse the
word "new" when describing such an unclassifiable work.
But the added word "necessary" was a definite falsehood, I
claimed, given the obvious contingency of the book's com-
position and even of Negarestani's own birth. China
countered (correctly, I knew) that this was the worst sort of
toying with words. By "necessary" he referred not to the
existence of the book itself, but to the timely cultural need
that it answered. In retribution he made a sally against my
own blurb for the work, which he remembered just as vividly:
"Reading Negarestani is like being converted to Islam by
Salvador Dali." China acknowledged the significant Islamic
themes of the work, but insisted with some vehemence that I
had merely pulled Dali's name from a hat, and that de Chirico
or Tanguy would have been keener analogies. This pointless

and basically insincere dispute ended only with our tacit decision to turn jointly on the third blurb from the book's back cover. Our chosen scapegoat was of course Nick Land, the former guru of the Warwick Deleuzians, now a self-imposed exile in Taiwan. Like a pair of hyenas we clawed at Land's printed behest to "Read Negarestani, and pray ..." For it was easy to reach consensus that this call to prayer was sheer affectation by Dr. Land, one of the noted atheists of his generation.

Once we were ready to change topics, we hit upon the idea of a memory contest. It was now almost three o'clock in the morning, and the wind was howling; amidst the sub-tropical gusts we drew straws, and mine was the shorter. As a model text I chose Poe's *Arthur Gordon Pym*, and proceeded impressively to recite the first two chapters of the work— or so I thought. For China was able to identify several embarrassing blunders in my recollection of the work, including the omission of the entire key paragraph beginning: "In the meantime, Henderson had again put off from the ship..."[13] For this unthinkable lapse I deserved the three minutes of mockery that came next, as China explored with relish the total collapse of plot that would result from such reckless editing. When I challenged him to do better, he selected Lovecraft's Antarctic tale "At the Mountains of Madness," a fitting riposte to Poe's own South Pole story. China's recitation was nearly perfect, and culminated in the famous dissection report quoted at the start of this chapter. The reader already knows that I failed to notice his slight mistakes with the numbers. Saluting his superior memory, I rose with a mock bow that was most inappropriate given the ongoing danger of wind and sea. But at least our tensions had ebbed, and we made common cause in an openly expressed wish to return to the mainland. We had already gathered sufficient atmospherics from this trip to fuel a half-dozen writing careers, and now wanted nothing more than sufficient safety to pursue those careers in peace.

As dawn approached, the hurricane seemed to have missed us. In fact we were just sixty minutes from rescue, though we could hardly have realized it at the time. Somewhat freed from despair, our conversation turned naturally toward metaphysics. China's views on the subject were of the materialist variety, and with the fingertips of dawn appearing on the eastern horizon, he made an eloquent speech in celebration of the dialectics of matter. Normally I would be pleased to reproduce his words here, but since they are almost sure to appear in the foreword to *Crisis Energy*, I do not wish to pre-empt his rights as an author. In response to China's speech, I followed my recently acquired habit of speaking in myth rather than argument: a dangerous vice that had already led to expulsion from the more rigorous philosophical circles in Heidelberg and London. The myth took offshore oil rigs as its topic, and went approximately as follows.

"We find ourselves on an offshore rig, guests of an industry on which all are dependent, yet which many thinking people view with disdain. The consumption of fuels is blamed for the decay of the climate and the impending doom of our species. You have heard my account of James Lovelock's appearance last April in Dublin, where he horrified the audience with his picture of the year 2100: a mere billion humans clustered in extreme northern climates and a few temperate refuges such as Ireland, New Zealand, and a severely reduced Albion and Japan. We both have minor doubts about this worst-case scenario, yet we have also cursed at least one oil-devouring vehicle on this trip. Let us bracket these judgments for now, and amuse ourselves instead with the machine on which we now sit. Drilling into the earth's crust far beneath the sea, it retrieves ancient materials from millions of years in the past. It draws them to the surface of everyday life, where they are used as energy for the most prosaic modern actions. The heating of a banal chain restaurant, like our stupefied movements from home to office, is possible only through combusting the remains of monstrous plants and animals that would destroy us in any personal encounter. Consider the strange carnivorous flowers, giant reptiles, and scurrying mammalian ancestors that were contemporaries of the oil now drawn from this platform.

"Now, imagine that instead of merely siphoning fuel for modern activities, these oil rigs had the power to draw full-blown ancient entities from the ground. Actual past species would be sucked from the earth, and we will assume that they come not only from the Jurassic and neighboring periods, but even from more recent human history. Egyptian deities, Grecian heroes, Hebrew prophets, Chinese rebels and warlords, Hunnish archers, the complete dialogues of Aristotle, early modern textiles, spices adored by Venetians, not to mention the obsolete technologies of our own childhood such as adding machines and antique toys— imagine that all these things could be drawn through tubes and pipes to this desolate platform in the Gulf of Mexico.

"Now that we have ascribed the power to this infernal machine of drawing all past things from the ground, we might also imagine it able to siphon *future* things into its sphere. Not that we ascribe divine foresight to the rig, or even that we believe the future to be predetermined, but that we imagine the oil rig to have a certain power of intelligent speculation that allows it to shuffle various permutations of future things. These would not merely be 'possible' things, but future things that are *actual* precisely insofar as the rig is thinking of them as images. From there it is a small step to deem the rig capable of siphoning all things occurring in the present as well. All elements of our current reality are now available for suction through pipes to the central brain of the platform: physical objects ranging in size from quarks and molecules to bars of iron, mountain ranges, and planets; social objects from herds of bison to international banks; various humans along with their bodily organs; fictional objects such as Othello, Popeye, or kryptonite. All of these entities are ready for transit through tubes to the mighty rig itself."

"We might imagine further that none of these past, present, or future things is capable of any direct connection with its neighbors. They are islands cut off from each other, so that only by means of the rig do they make even indirect contact. You already know that this theory is called occasionalism. Some of the Arabs of Iraq had theological reasons for barring causal relations to any entity other than God. And in Europe from Descartes forward, there was a metaphysical reason for saying so— namely, the worry that mental and physical substance would be unable to interact. In the myth now under discussion I propose that we secularize the concept to the verge of blasphemy, replacing the *Ens Perfectissimum* who created the cosmos with as crass a physical object as an offshore oil platform. Why? Because this substitution helps make things more vivid. And besides, many political critics already contend that oil controls the world, and hence the image is more plausible than most alternatives. Furthermore, the known ability of oil rigs to siphon entities from distant times and spaces adds additional weight to the myth.

"It should not be imagined that the rig is capable of summoning all past, present, and future things in their own right. Instead, it draws forth *images* of them. For the rig is by no means limitless in power. It cares nothing for the smell of the rose or the nuanced characters of the living humans drawn through its tubes. For the rig, each of these things still has a far simpler reality: its capacity to serve as marketable fuel. The role of God in past occasionalisms suppressed this limitation, since no faithful person would concede any reality lying beyond the exhaustive knowledge of God. But in the case of a mere oil rig, all will admit the frailty of its knowledge. Even the mightiest barons of oil do not take it for divine; instead, they ruthlessly exploit the fluid for selfish purposes. In any case, China, you are a famous writer of science fiction. You of all people will find it easy to reflect on a dystopia in which a single oil rig is connected via trillions of suction tubes to all past, present, and future objects, while also monopolizing their interactions." From the corner of my eye I first saw China nodding, but then I saw the gleam of sarcasm in his eye. He pointed vaguely in turn to each of the other rigs on the horizon, and I could see his lips mouthing a count: "seven ... eight ... nine ..." And this led directly to the next part of my myth.

"Your thoughts are known to me. And I will admit that this platform on which we now sit is no better than any of the dozens of others in the vicinity. Hence it would be absurd to select just one of these mediocre rigs to play the role of God in our philosophy, while arbitrarily excluding the others as mere agglomerations of iron and wood. Thus I propose a brief experiment with a philosophy never attempted by the most heretic Muslim or deviant Frenchman. The model I propose is an occasionalist *polytheism*. Rather than a single oil rig mediating all interactions in the cosmos, we imagine a division of labor between all forty or fifty rigs that lie near us. Like the gods who take opposite sides at Troy and interfere with each other's plans, these rigs will intervene as they please in siphoning objects through their tubes. And remember that there is plenty of room for this to occur, since we do not imagine any rig siphoning an object fully and irreplaceably from its place in the cosmos, but insist that it only draws images from the things. There are as many images of each object as there are rigs that encounter them. Fifty rigs could all siphon the same cat, for instance, and the result would simply be fifty different cat-images, with the cat itself possibly remaining untouched by the exercise.

"Perhaps you see where I am leading. For if we abandon the occasionalist God in favor of an oil rig, and then abandon a single all-powerful rig in favor of a vast legion of equipotent divine platforms, why stop there? Why not grant *all* objects the power to act as oil rigs, each draining phantasmal energy from all of the others? We can literally imagine all rabbits, monkeys, electrons, acids, and freight trains as equipped with pipes and tubing of their own. All real objects of every size now have the power to interact with all other things, at the price of turning them into images. The entire cosmos is in fact a dystopia filled with trillions of miniature deities, each of them a platform in a hurricane-infested gulf. Woe to the cosmos that generates such a legion of corrupt entities, reducing all other things to the equivalent of oil for burning. The tragedy of it! The hell of existence itself! Yet there is little alternative to viewing the universe in precisely this way. Certainly your own books have considered many notions at least as strange. And hence, friend, I fear no limits on your imagination in what follows.

"Already we have encountered the first of three key features of causation. Years ago during my studies in Chicago, I made the fateful decision to abandon the term 'occasional cause,' despite my great fondness for this under-rated historical current— the first in history to grant beings total autonomy from one another, if not from God. Instead, I spoke of *vicarious* causation. A vicar is the earthly represen-tative of something that need not act in person. But the same must be true of causation itself. The genius of occasionalism was to cut things off from one another to such an extent that only God could link them. The solution was clearly outlandish, its vagueness protected from scrutiny only by the shield of piety, since the mechanisms of direct Divine contact were never explained. But at least this model grasped that things have a certain rigorous independence from one another. And while occasionalism is subject to ridicule today, it is surely no worse than the more popular solutions of Hume and Kant. These idolized kingpins of the present-day academy merely replace the almighty God with an almighty human whose habits and categories monopolize causation no less than Allah or Jehovah was once allowed to do." And here China nodded vaguely in agreement, though with visible unease. I proceeded in the same spirit as before:

"We have seen that causation is *vicarious*. Like oil rigs reducing all other entities to fuel, each object reduces every other to a hazy caricature of its deeper plenitude. But now I want to show why causation must also be *asymmetrical*. To a materialist like you, I realize the claim will sound absurd. For in materialism all objects operate on the same plane of reality. If two entities collide, then both collide with each other, not just one with the other. 'Every action has an equal and opposite reaction,' in the familiar Newtonian phrase. The materialist will admit that the moon has less force on the sun than the reverse, but will also insist that *some* interaction must occur in both directions. Yet this is precisely what I contest.

"Consider the action of the offshore rig as it siphons mere images of all that it touches. Even a friendly critic of my philosophy such as Levi Bryant (you know of his blog[14] and his struggles with ignorant trolls) rejects this asymmetry, though he concedes that nothing exists but *translation*. In agreement with Latour's philosophy, Bryant contends that no thing makes contact with another without transforming it.

Yet he still holds that my theory of withdrawn objects and vicarious causation is too extreme. As I see it, what Bryant and Latour both miss is that translation is also a starting point, not just a result. That is to say, the point is not that fire makes easy contact with cotton, or a horse with a meadow, and that they *then* translate or distort these entities in accordance with their own perspectives. This would imply an initial direct contact, with a sort of indirect translation then pasted on as a supplement. Instead, I claim that even the initial contact between two entities is only the contact of a real entity with a translated or phenomenal one. The real entity is certainly there: for instance, it is not an *image* of me that lives in the world and encounters various things, but the *real* me. By the same token it is a real fire that has effects in the world, not an imaginary one. Yet never do any two real things make contact. Even inanimate reality is an asymmetrical world of real entities making contact with phenomenal ones. Direct contact is no more found at the outset than in the result. Translation is no psychological quirk of unlucky humans whose mentality cannot probe the depths of things; rather, it belongs to the very stuff of relation. For causation to be vicarious means by the same stroke that it must be asymmetrical as well.

"And this brings us to a third property of causation: namely, it is *buffered*. A thing does not come from the void and strike us like a meteor. This model also reflects one of the many prejudices of materialism. Namely, it holds that contact between two entities is an all-or-nothing affair, with entities first at a distance and then suddenly striking us as if from nowhere. In fact, a more rudimentary form of contact must always be present before deeper contact is made at a level beyond that of images. Even in what is called 'love at first sight' there must be a minimal instant in which we are in contact with the beloved before love takes effect. What I mean is that things can be in contact with something else without being *fully* in contact with them, just as the philosopher loves wisdom without fully possessing it. Our initial state is that of a hazy half-contact with the images of things. These images may shift or warble slightly, but this need not have any resulting effect on the world. The landscape of entities remains stable: perception is purely a matter of phantoms. Only now and then does this situation break down and lead to two real objects indirectly affecting one another by means of a third. And this is one form of what I call 'allure.' Consider the case of artworks ..."

But here I was interrupted— and not by China, who had listened attentively despite his materialist suspicion toward my words. Rather, my phrase was cut off by the sound of a helicopter bearing the markings of the United States Navy. We burst out shouting: "We're saved! We're saved!" and laughed aloud like a pair of decades-long castaways, though we had been stranded alone on the platform for just eighteen miserable hours. Leaping in triumph and deliverance, we both reached for objects to wave in the air, and both found strange banners to hold aloft in gratitude. China's flag was of a deep green, bearing a stylized emblem suggesting the form of sugar cane. But my own flag was even more unsettling: on a field of burgundy, poppies struck by hail.

5

The Haunted Boat

Allow me to recall a scene from my childhood. Some of the happiest days of my early life were spent at the home of grandparents in the Chicago suburb of Northbrook. The place was a wonderland for children, with dozens of toys and sudden hot lunches, along with the extensive media resources that only a large city like Chicago commands. But I wish to speak here of a single recurrent incident from those days. One afternoon in Northbrook I awoke from a nap to be told by my brother that I had just missed a visit from "Officer Vic." This was the name of a supposed policeman who would land his helicopter in the neighborhood, making speeches to children and passing out chocolate and balloons. This news from my brother was no isolated incident. He had often reported such stories of Officer Vic during the years of our shared youth, though coincidence always prevented my ever seeing the man myself. In our conversations and our games, the elusive officer was frequently invoked as a mythic protector, and even identified with a generic toy policeman in our possession. At times I was suspicious of his existence, given that his landings always coincided with my naps or rare absences from the home. It is true that our grandmother endorsed my brother's story on at least one occasion. But while she was never known to speak deception, she was of a sufficiently sweet disposition as to have told a "noble lie" to allow my brother to save face among his peers. Now that we have reached adulthood, I could surely count on a frank reply if I were to ask my brother point-blank whether the officer was a fabrication. Yet I find myself disinclined to do so: less through a fear of feeling duped in retrospect than from unwillingness to lose yet another Santa Claus from the depleted pantheon of childhood. Such ruined temples are no laughing matter, but are borne by everyone as a crippling burden across the years.

The point of remembering Officer Vic is that I faced a similar predicament years later, in Japan. For academic and business reasons I made a long stay in Hiroshima, a lively city now filled with joy despite its infamous catastrophe. Early in my stay a Canadian friend wrote to say he was staying with his Japanese wife in Matsuyama, on the eastern island of Shikoku. With gratitude I accepted his invitation, and was received in the warmest possible fashion; a tour of the hilltop castle was a highlight despite the ceaseless rain. More importantly, through this trip I became a devotee of the ferry route between Hiroshima and Matsuyama, and made the return journey dozens of times in the weeks that followed. Naturally, such frequent travel habits led me to notice other regular commuters, and an outgoing person like me could hardly fail to befriend a number of fellow passengers. One of these was a pleasant native of Osaka, roughly my own age, who said that his name was Kenji. An engineer by training, and normally given to hardheaded critique of all supernatural things, he seemed strangely credulous about the supposed existence of a "haunted boat" in these waters of the Inland Sea. It was said to be a small fishing trawler of antiquated appearance. Several disturbing features of the boat had given it the reputation of being haunted. It rode unnaturally high in the water and moved with unexpected speed in apparent silence; it was able to change directions quickly, and would sometimes remain motionless for unusual periods of time. On other occasions it would dart close to a passenger ferry in a somewhat threatening manner. A loud horn of warning would then be sounded by the ferry captain, and this would usually chase the haunted boat away. At all times, amorphous white shapes could be seen flashing behind the portholes just below the deck. While not universally known to the Japanese public, the story was backed by solid oral tradition on Shikoku and the facing areas of Kyushu and Honshu. The first time he told me the story, Kenji readily admitted never having seen the boat. But over the next few weeks, he claimed to have observed it on several occasions. In a suspicious manner harking back to the tale of Officer Vic, this haunted boat always seemed to appear at times when I was napping above deck.

On these occasions Kenji always claimed either that he could not find me or, alternatively, that he did not wish to disturb my rest. Each time he reported a new sighting of the boat, a few elements of the tale were added or dropped. But one portion of the story that never varied was his account of a strange incantation from its deck, repeated several times in succession. On each repetition the vowels of the words would change, though the consonants were obviously the same. The language was said to be neither Japanese nor any Asian tongue. While Kenji could not be sure, the experience of several journeys in Europe led him to conjecture that it was one of the Slavic languages other than Russian. While I might have asked another passenger to verify these stories, Kenji told his tales in such a hushed whisper that I feared making them public fact. And unlike my brother, who can still be consulted about Officer Vic at a moment of my choosing, Kenji is now dead (or so I read recently on his suspended Facebook page). In all the ensuing years I have assumed that the haunted boat still prowls Japanese waters, and reports of Kenji's death have only heightened my interest in the vessel, not to mention my fear of it. Having never seen the boat in person, I am left with nothing but idle speculation. Yet the following myth is the only way I can make sense of the boat, and I like to think that the lamented Kenji would have been pleased by my theory.

It seems possible, if unlikely, that such a boat exists. The prevalence of ghosts in Asian tradition is widely known; among my Vietnamese friends, even the most highly trained engineers swear to first-hand sightings. This fact has led some to reduce the phenomenon to a matter of culture. But this neglects the real possibility of unequal distribution of ghosts along the earth's surface; perhaps something about Asia is welcoming to these lonely spirits. And given longstanding tradition that ghosts are generated by sudden or violent deaths, no one could doubt that Hiroshima might be enveloped in a haze of phantoms, however happy the city may be today. Nor will anyone doubt the crucial role of *boats* in such cultures. In Japanese tradition alone, we find associations of various gods with the treasure boat and fishing rod. There is the myth of Oikumuri and Samai-unkur and their long fishing trips, on which they encounter the North Wind (in the form of a goddess) and are dragged for days by a swordfish, until it dies of a curse and is eaten by birds and land creatures.[15] It is true that Kenji's ghost boat has never been found, but this is easily explained by the lack of organized searches: unlike Scotland's Loch Ness Monster, that probably fraudulent creature that eludes detection by sonar and satellite, the Haunted Boat has never been tracked with vigor. Moreover, the Inland Sea of Japan is not landlocked at all, but a genuine branch of the ocean, so that no *ad hoc* tunnels or concealed lairs are needed of the kind dreamed up for the beast of Loch Ness. The Haunted Boat could easily retreat to Puerto Princesa in the Philippines (with its sunless river beneath the earth's crust) or hide out far at sea. Or given its ghostly status, it might simply dematerialize at will. Whatever it is, I will suppose the boat to be a purely Asian phenomenon, and dismiss Kenji's speculations about the use of a Slavic tongue as a simple mishearing. For although he gave surprisingly little physical description of the boat, he left the impression that it was basically Japanese in shape: constructed in modified flatboat style, not the Western model of spinal cord and ribs.

But in a sense the visual appearance of the haunted boat is beside the point; its shape and color alone reveal nothing out of the ordinary. Instead, there is something vaguely amiss in the boat's *mode of being*. But to clarify this phrase requires some actual philosophy. In this spirit we will forget the haunted boat for a moment, and consider instead the Hiroshima-Matsuyama ferry from whose deck it was reportedly witnessed. Surely no one makes supernatural claims for the ferry. It is a mere prosaic watercraft that may afford charming panoramas, but is nothing more than an assemblage of physical pieces. It has an exact industrial history traceable to a specific shipyard, and to a contractor now under indictment. The captain and crew of the ferry were delightful people, but had nothing of the magical about them. They struck me as mainstream nautical workers, lacking the usual personal quirks that one would expect of a ghost story. And it is good that the boat turns out to be so banal, since philosophy must be capable of dealing with everyday objects like these, not just with eerie borderline cases.

Philosophy took a great step forward, barely noticed, when Edmund Husserl discovered a tension in objects between their identity and their shifting multitude of traits. For Husserl the Matsuyama ferry would not be explained in mechanical terms according to the physical forces by which it is constructed and propelled. This natural reality of the boat should be suspended or "bracketed," turning the boat into an appearance to be explored, without judgment on that part of it which lies beyond the mind. In this way, the school of phenomenology was launched. Instead of describing the ferry as composed of steel and wood, engines and hydraulics, we examine its various modulations before the mind. We consider that the boat as a whole is never visible, but present only through simplified faces; we analyze the precise inter-action of its surface contours with my memories and moods. Whatever the benefits of this method, an accursed idealism lies at its core, since the reality of the boat-in-itself is excluded from discussion. This must be condemned, and Husserl's realist critics have not refrained from condemning it: he has now replaced Plato as the most unjustly treated of our great philosophers.

Now, the typical educated view of phenomenal reality is guided largely by the seventeenth and eighteenth century dogmas of British Empiricism. In the eyes of this tradition we do not encounter a ferry, but only a certain number of impres-sions or qualities in isolation from each other. Largely through the force of habit, or "customary conjunction," we find these qualities assembled together so often that we begin to compress them into unified bundles. What we call "the ferry" is really just a nickname for a set of qualities encoun-tered together directly. By contrast, Husserl's great discovery was that experience is not made of qualities; instead, it is made of *objects*. Yet his objects are not real things lying beyond the phenomenal realm: for Husserl, it is absurd to proclaim a reality that would exist without being in principle the possible target of some conscious act. There is no cryptic ferry withdrawing into the shadows of Being, but only the visible ferry as encountered by consciousness. Despite this lack of realism in Husserl's position, his ferry is no bundle of qualities, but a unified object. Notice that its qualities shift constantly: the ferry rocks differently in the waves at every moment, and we always see it from a specific angle from a definite height above the deck. But notwithstanding all these constant shifts, I continue to see it as one and the same boat. There can be no question of whether I am right or wrong in these perceptions, because we are now speaking only of the life of phenomena in the mind, regardless of whether they manage to copy a real world outside. The latter notion plays no role in Husserl's philosophy at all. Instead of the boat being the sum of its palpable qualities, such qualities emanate from a boat that is unified in advance; they would appear quite different if we encountered them elsewhere. In short, there is a tension in Husserl between phenomenal objects and their phenomenal qualities. The "objects" side of this pair is genuine for Husserl, and not a bundled byproduct of the "qualities" side.

But there is a second tension in Husserl as well. For notice that the Matsuyama ferry, which endures despite all its swirling facades, is not just an empty pole of unity. Instead, it has a highly specific character different from that of the waves, the clouds, and the leaping dolphins of the Inland Sea. If for the most part we grasp the character of the ferry vaguely and inarticulately, we also have the ability to analyze it. And this is what Husserl calls the "eidetic reduction": through analysis, we try to determine what features are truly required by the ferry in order to be what it is, rather than a dog, tree, or dolphin. Yet there is the strange paradox that Husserl does not regard these "eidetic" features of the ferry as having the same sort of reality that its sensual features do. In other words, he does not suggest that we sift through all our impressions of the boat and choose an elite five percent of them to be crucial while dismissing the other ninety-five percent as disposable. Instead, the eidetic qualities of an object can *never* be sensibly present. None of the pivotal features of the ferry can ever be made visible: they are "categorial" rather than sensual. And just as the ferry is not a bundle of sensual qualities, neither is it a bundle of eidetic ones. These eidetic qualities radiate vaguely from the analyzed thing, never graspable by the senses. But they are not like sticks that might be glued together to form a sensual object. In this way we find a second great tension in Husserl's thinking: that between sensual objects and *real* qualities. The important qualities of the ferry are real because they exist independently of our access to them, though the ferry itself does not; they hide from every view and are encountered only obliquely. True enough, Husserl does not fully emphasize this inaccessible hiddenness of the qualities of things. Indeed, he often insists that categorial intuition provides *direct* access to reality in a way that the senses do not. Yet this misleading claim is merely the sad consequence of his idealism, which allows no reality outside of possible presence to consciousness. And we need not follow him here.

To this discussion we now invite Martin Heidegger, Husserl's rebellious and more famous student. One contrast immediately becomes clear: in Heidegger's thinking there is plenty of room for real objects. In his illustrious tool-analysis, he denies Husserl's claim that our primary mode of dealing with things is being conscious of them. Instead, we deal with things by taking them for granted, using them in a way that is anything but conscious. We tend to notice them mostly when they fail: not the flawless hammer or the reliable bus route, but the failed, degenerate versions of these tools. If Husserl draws a distinction between the ferry in consciousness and its various shifting profiles, Heidegger considers the ferry as *withdrawn* from all conscious access. For Husserl the ferry is always available, and simply encrusted with noisy accidents that vary without cease; by contrast, Heidegger's ferry is concealed from any human encounter. And here we have the third tension, found in Heidegger but never in Husserl: the difference between a withdrawn real object and the accessible, sensual crust through which it is known. Nor can we forget a fourth tension silently present in Heidegger's work— though given his tendency to melt all concealed objects into a pre-Socratic whole, it is found more clearly in Leibniz's *Monadology*[16] or Xavier Zubíri's remarkable post-Heideggerian philosophy.[17] Real objects, no less than sensual ones, are torn between their unified reality and their plurality of specific traits. They are not empty poles of unity, but have distinct qualities without being mere bundles. And thus we have the fourth tension in things.

Returning briefly to the case of the ferry, we can spell out in greater detail how the four tensions work. The first tension is between the ferry as we know it and its multitude of shifting traits. It rocks from side to side, viewed in sun and gloom, covered by salt spray or crossed by dry summer wind; it is viewed while standing or crouching, in both joy and despair. This tension in which a unified thing of the senses emits a sandstorm of shifting facades is what we mean by *time*. The time we experience involves precisely this landscape of constantly swirling accidents atop some minimally enduring core: the sensual objects. That was the first tension described above, and we call it time. Through Husserl's hard work we also saw that the ferry-object begins as a vague if compelling unit, but that it can also be analyzed into genuine traits rather than the noisily swirling ones of the senses. This tension is what Husserl calls the *eidos* (in a different sense from Plato's). It is a tension between the sensual objects of experience and the features they truly need to exist, though in the case of sensual objects that existence must be for some perceiver.

Returning to Heidegger we also recall the third tension, in which all visible features of the ferry are in tension not only with a *sensual* ferry, but also with a *real* one that withdraws into darkness and remains invisible no matter how much it malfunctions. There is no better name for this third tension than *space*. Although it is sometimes said that space is a system of relations, this can only be a half-truth: for space is clearly the system of both relations *and* non-relations. While the boat is related to Calcutta and Montevideo as possible ports of call, it is not currently in those places: instead, it withholds itself in coy reserve in Japanese waters. In short, space is the name for the fact that things fail to be in direct contact without being outside all contact entirely. The real ferry is withdrawn from us, and hence is spatially distinct from us. This is the primary meaning of space, compared to which the quantified space of three dimensions is derivative. The fourth tension, ascribed by us to Heidegger but far more explicit in Leibniz, lies between the real subterranean ferry and its subterranean features. And in classical terms, this tension between a thing's unified reality and its multitude of features is best called *essence*. In the ferry, then, as in all other things, we encounter a fourfold structure of time, space, essence, and eidos. No longer are time and space pampered twin sisters freed from all other rivals in metaphysics and popular imagination. Instead they are merely half of a set of quadruplets, reunited with their unknown sisters essence and eidos. Yet the banality of the world is such that only rarely do we notice these tensions. Though we are well aware that a boat, candle, or donkey can be seen from many different angles, we tend to fuse these unified entities lazily with their shifting sensual contours. The same holds for their eidos, their essence, and their spatial withholding from all other things. For the most part time, space, essence, and eidos function in brutally dull fashion. We certainly see this in the case of the ferry, which one day will bore us despite the surrounding beauty of mountains, sea, and dolphins.

And here at last we must summon the haunted boat once more, having dwelled too long on the crushing normalcy of the ferry. My notion is that the ghost boat was dispatched by the gods of Shinto to restore some philosophy to this tired cosmos. For with ghosts, no banality is possible. Whereas a normal ferry merely rotates perspectives while passing us, the haunted boat moves jumpily at unusual speed and with odd pauses as it rides high in the water. This forces us to *confront* the tension between the unified haunted boat and its multitude of shifting features. Let "confrontation" be the name for those sporadic cases where we come directly to grips with the difference between a thing and its slippery sensual traits. The haunted boat also provokes us to a certain theoretical labor. We do not take the genuine features of the boat for granted as we often do for the regular ferry, but must work very hard to unlock its eidos. We form a *theory* about it, and theory is what disrupts the usual dull bond between the sensual object and its real hidden traits. Further, we can also say that the boat is alluring— haunting our dreams and luring us toward our doom. To conceive this thing prowling the waters of Japan has altered my world, perhaps even for the worse. The mechanics of this *allure* can be found in many places, but especially so in the case of ghosts: instead of the normal relation between a withdrawn real thing and its sensual surface traits, a ghost suggests a certain ungraspable spirit lying beyond all access. Indeed, all beauty has something ghostly about it. Finally, there is the fourth tension between the real hidden ghost boat and its real hidden features. When the normal relation between the haunted boat and its features is disrupted, then we have a transference of properties between things. These are cases of *causation*, and causation does not occur at every moment. Under normal circumstances, the boat may continue as it was for long periods without anything ever happening.

And in this respect the current myth differs from those we heard earlier. The image of a giant ferris wheel first occupied us at life-sized scale, but eventually we found that the metaphor worked all the way up and down the ladder of the cosmos. All objects have the same structure as a ferris wheel, including the most unspeakably tiny entities. The same turned out to be true of the calliope, whose mutating features are no more variable than those of trees or dogs; the myth had a universal scope, with all objects now seen as frightening musical instruments. And most blatantly of all, there was the vision of a horrific cosmos in which all entities were viewed as competing rigs draining oil from one another. By contrast, the myth of the haunted boat is not universal. Although even boring ferries *can* split along their four axes, this does not mean that they constantly *are* splitting in this manner. And I well recall that Kenji's prayers from the *Yengishiki* were always addressed specifically to the many ships on the sea, not the many atoms in the void.

6

The Sleeping Zebra

The philosopher Bruno Latour is an excellent host to those who visit his flat in the Latin Quarter of Paris. The son of an established wine dynasty, he always has several bottles of Corton on hand to share with guests. Those who wish it may even be offered an after-dinner cigar. But the latter offer is no longer extended to me on visits to the rue Danton, since Latour is well aware of my fondness for only one means of smoking: the *shisha*, that apple-scented goddess of the Near East. On one occasion at his home, we were speaking of this venerable device of Akbar's Mughal court, when my thoughts turned to the clouds of *smoke* that emanate from the pipe. By association, the idea of smoke led at once to the closely related notion of *steam*. And when thinking of this word in the presence of Bruno Latour, I could hardly fail to remember "Why Has Critique Run Out of Steam?," his 2003 Presidential Lecture at Stanford University, later published in *Critical Inquiry*.[18] Sitting in armchairs on a creaky wooden floor (and as always, without background music) we carried on a lengthy discussion of this stimulating lecture, with whose basic principles I fully agree. Latour was in a listening mood, and politely allowed me to expound on the recent mutation of the critic into the full-fledged *troll*: that despicable stock character of the unmonitored salt flats of the internet. My thesis was that the troll is the new successor to past figures of anti-philosophy: the sophist, the pedant, and the Inquisitor, among others. I argued that the troll is the degenerate form of the critic, untethered from any commitment of his own, and unleashed on the world to doubt and critique whatever one *might* doubt and critique rather than what truly deserves refutation. The full version of my argument will soon appear in an edited volume, and hence I will not belabor it here. The point is this: Latour and I found ourselves in agreement on the decadent state of critical method today. Where we still disagreed was on whether an object might be real even if it had no effect on anything else, or indeed no relation to anything else at all. This dispute between us had been established years earlier, and generally followed a well-worn path.

On this occasion we both hoped for a new twist on our friendly old trench war. But we were not forty-five minutes into the discussion when Latour received a call from one of his staff at Sciences-Po, as the Institut d'Études Politiques de Paris is affectionately known. The matter was said to be urgent, and Latour excused himself, inviting me to make myself at home for the next hour or two as he resolved the difficulties at the office. He then departed on foot for the rue Saint-Guillaume, and I drank with pleasure from my glass of Louis Latour, trying to conceive some innovation, some brilliant compromise that would settle our amicable dispute over the duel of objects and relations. It was unusually cold for a spring day, and the gusts of wind had been sudden and jarring through the afternoon. Approximately one hour after Latour's departure, there began a powerful hailstorm. At first the hail was barely worthy of the name: harmless pellets resembling the stuffing of a beanbag chair. But in the familiar manner of such storms, the stones became larger until they finally reached terrifying size. At that point a car alarm began to sound nearby on the rue Danton itself, and an eerie, quavering whistle arose in the distance— a sound I would later hear in the office of a literary agent. Only now did I notice three strange flags hanging from poles on the building across the street. The leftmost banner showed a jagged green triangle on a field of deep vermillion. The flag on the right was less visible under current wind conditions, but was evidently an optical illusion employing a tightly wound spiral. But it was the flag in the center that would play a major role in my day: this banner showed a lifelike zebra on a background of purest azure. Something seemed familiar about this sleeping animal, and I soon recalled once using a zebra as an example for my theory of dormant or sleeping objects. It was on this theory that I now reflected, continuing my efforts to find some point of mediation between Latour's philosophy (which allowed for no sleeping objects) and my own (which flatly demanded them).

It must have been the excessive quantities of burgundy that pushed me into deep sleep despite the violence of the hailstorm. Soon I was dreaming, and the reader will be surprised to hear that the dream was made up entirely of a beginner's course in *set theory*. The muse Thalia appeared in her smiling mask, and urged me to practice this art. With fire and eloquence she contended that ontology and mathematics were the same, and even frightened me with her oracular maxims about the empty set. In the early portions of the dream I moved with ease over vast portions of the discipline, in the compressed and satisfying manner that only dreams allow. Generally I was most at ease when confined to the notions of Peano and Russell, though in waking life I had barely studied these figures. Yet when Thalia began to speak of the Zermelo-Fraenkel theorems endorsed by the philosophy of Badiou, my heart grew panicked. Thalia seemed to be laughing, and I felt myself sinking deeper into the sandy plain on which I stood, as a dying red sun showered me with lethal radiation. But here things took a turn for the better. From somewhere off to my left came a voice that was first heard barely through static, as if transmitted from a distant stellar probe. From this scratchy initial condition, the voice became more mechanical in tone, like that of a cyborg crying for aid. And finally it took shape as the calming voice of Professor Hallward, another non-specialist in the field, whose book on Badiou[19] had admirably clarified the basic principles of sets. Having thereby escaped the betrayal by Thalia, I slipped into a further deep sleep within the dream itself.

At this I awoke to the reality of Paris once more. The hailstorm was still underway. As I gazed out the window, the flag with the sleeping zebra was fully unfurled in the wind before my eyes, and I imagined a myth involving that flag, hoping to test it on Latour after his return. For various reasons it later slipped my mind, and to this day he has never heard it. But the myth went roughly as follows.

The core of my philosophy is the notion that objects cannot encounter each other directly, an idea derived from my reading of Heidegger's notorious tool-beings.[20] His tools are misread if we take them for handy utensils involved in praxis prior to theory, since the point is that practical action fails to exhaust the reality of things *no less* than theory does. The mere act of sitting in a chair does not grasp its nature any more than conscious debates about that chair. Since tools withdraw into darkness beyond all access, we are left to encounter a realm of phenomenal presence, entirely different in kind from the underground zone of concealment. Human life is adrift in a sensual realm. But we have seen that this realm is not formed of detached sparks of quality pressed into a bundle by the habits of the mind. Instead the sensual landscape is quantized, split into objects as if into chunks; the world of the senses is by no means purely a continuum. Against correspondence theories of truth, none of these sensual or intentional objects are an accurate match for the real things of which they are only translations, distortions, or caricatures. The next strange step is to see that nonhuman objects must do this to each other as well. To meet with a phenomenal realm is not the unique burden of the exceptional human or animal brain: rather, it is the very stuff of relation. For not just animal mentality is condemned to translate its objects, to meet only phenomenal objects from the start. The same is true even of material things, which cannot slap one another directly, and hence deal with each other only in mediated form. All things, both human and nonhuman, must encounter other things in the form of sensual caricatures: for the sole alternative would be a direct form of contact that we have seen to be impossible.

This has led to the charge that I project human features too deeply into the non-human sphere. After all, we only know that *sentient* creatures perceive, and to ascribe this same ability to the inanimate realm sounds like the work of animists and cranks. The position is dismissed as a panpsychist vitalism that ignores the difference between humans and non-humans. I answer that my critics are the ones truly at fault. For it is they who posit the groundless dogma that the representations of animal mind are absolutely opposed to blind and direct physical contact. But projecting mind into matter, or calling matter the root of mind, are equally miserable options. Both take the lazy approach of reducing one realm to another. But if reduction is really needed, it makes more sense to notice that causation and consciousness share something deeper: namely, both are *relations*. And given that relations cannot take the form of direct contact between real entities, which are always mutually withdrawn, they can only be indirect relations. And this entails that they encounter only what we call sensual, phenomenal, or intentional objects. The landscape of sensual things must be imagined in a primitive sense that does not imply high-grade human or animal access to the phenomenal realm, such as thought, memory, fantasy, dreams, and the like. Yet the sentient sphere is merely different in degree, not in kind, from the primordial kingdom where dust collides with dirt.

The charge of panpsychism is admittedly somewhat credible. But while I have warmed to the label in recent years, it is not strictly accurate here. For panpsychists hold that all things have psyche as soon as they *exist*, and I claim instead that they have psyche as soon as they *relate*. It is by no means the case that existing and relating are one and the same. This erroneous notion comes from the failure to distinguish between those relations that generate a thing and the further relations in which it itself takes part. Against Leibniz, the myth of the calliope claimed that while everything is unified, nothing is simple. All that exists is composed of pieces, and obviously these must relate in order for the thing itself to exist; everything must first be aggregate in order to become substance. But note that the thing already exceeds these constituent relations in some way. For instance, the components of my body change constantly without my always becoming different as a result. It is true that a point may be reached where this change in pieces is sufficient to destroy me. Yet that point must actually be reached; it is not attained automatically with every slight shift in the infrastructure of human and inhuman things.

But whatever degree of autonomy a thing has from its own pieces, its independence increases vastly when we move upward— considering objects as the *source* rather than the product of relations. Objects move easily from one predicament to another, none of them exhausting their inherent reality. While outside events might destroy or alter the character of the object with diseases, fires, or bombs, it is by no means necessary that they do so. Sometimes, nothing happens. And if an object can exist apart from any specific situation, it can also exist apart from any situation at all. This will be denied at first, but only because we tend to think of objects in purely physical terms, and physical objects always exist in some particular position in the environment. Yet there may be other objects that do have real parts that make them real things, but still have no relation to anything further; precisely for this reason, they will currently have no psyche. We might call them "dormant objects," a notion excluded in advance by every relationist philosophy. The dormant is the sleeping, and though perfect sleep may be impossible for dreamers like us, nightly sleep is our closest approach to the freedom from relation in which we are most ourselves. Perhaps God is not the most alert of all beings, but rather the most oblivious.

And thus we return to the image of the sleeping zebra, inaccessible to the hailstones that vainly attempted to wake it. In Chapter 2 above, the pre-Socratic thinkers were condemned to death; though the penalty was harsh, their crime cannot be denied. All of these thinkers embraced reductive philosophies, leading all objects back toward some primordial alpha factor: the formless *apeiron* for some; water, air, numbers, or atoms for others. These charming elements were depicted as permanent features of reality, and all more intricate things as mere transient constellations of tiny or primary roots. It was Aristotle who first paid respect to everyday individual things. But while avoiding the reductive maneuvers of the pre-Socratics, he adds one of his own, by contending that only *one* level of realities exists. Humans are substance, but societies are not; animals are substance, but herds of animals are not. We must reject this bias as false. The zebra is real, its sub-pieces down to infinity are real, and the successive menageries and herds it joins might often be equally real. We do not claim that no difference exists between substance and aggregate, since a random collection of things need not be real or one: perhaps all herds are excluded from being unified realities. We claim only that the difference is not clear or absolute; the zebra can be both substance and aggregate at the same time. It is something over and above its pieces, for it has qualities that these pieces do not have, and not every change in these pieces transforms the zebra itself. The creature remains the same even when some of its atoms are vaporized or shuffled.

For the great relational ontologies of the past century, an entity is composed of both its inner and outer relations: both the pieces that give rise to it, and the effects it has on other things. The zebra is made equally of its own pieces and of its impact on other objects. Sometimes an effort is made to say in Whitehead's defense that the two strands are disconnected: the zebra as already constituted has a "subjective aim," thereby giving it a certain autonomy from the various possible networks into which it might now enter.[21] But this is not enough. For the real asymmetry is found not between the inside and outside of the zebra, but between the zebra itself on the one hand and *both* its inside and outside on the other. For first, it rises beyond its own pieces, generated by them but not reducible to them. And second, it is indifferent to the various negotiations into which it might enter with other objects, though some of these may affect it: as when the zebra interacts with grasses for its meals, and predator cats for its doom. While the zebra is cut off from its pieces in the sense of being partly immune to changes among them, it cannot survive their total disappearance. But by contrast, it might well survive the disappearance of *all* its outward relations. And this is what I mean by sleep, if we can imagine a truly deep and dreamless sleep. One will object that the zebra does not vanish from the world while sleeping, for even in the case of a perfect sleep it still lies on the savanna, in contact with its environment. But I would counter that this is no longer the zebra; rather, in this case it is the *pieces* of the zebra that remain in relation to the world, while the zebra itself perhaps withdraws completely from the world. Sleep should not be compared with death and its genuine destruction of the zebra-entity: sleep entails that the thing still exists, but simply without relation to anything else. Consider how important sleep is for the vital functions, making up roughly a third of our time on this planet, some of it approaching a deep and dreamless state. Sleep perhaps has a metaphysical function no less than a physical one: as a kind of suspended animation in which entities are withdrawn from the world. And perhaps this happens more often than we think.

As stated above, panpsychism holds that everything perceives as soon as it exists. I counter that everything perceives only insofar as it *relates*. To perceive something obviously requires some sort of relation with it. But there are more terms at work in such a relation than is commonly believed. Namely, when the zebra perceives the abandoned campfire of poachers, we have seen that this object is merely phenomenal or sensual. It would be easy to regard this experience, and all others, as occurring on the inside of a *mind*: that of the zebra. But recall that the zebra's mind is just one ingredient in this situation, and the campfire another; the mind cannot be both part of the situation *and* the whole of it. The encounter between zebra and fire is not just two things, but also one: the experience as a whole. And when something is one, it instantly acquires the status of "object." Despite our bias that objects must be solid physical things, such solids are only a special case of objects in general. If something is one, and has a reality that resists any perception from outside, then it deserves to be called an object. This joint zebra-fire entity contains both the real zebra and the sensual fire. Often, but not always, there may be a parallel entity that contains the reverse: real fire and sensual zebra. In short, to perceive is to be a piece of a larger relation: the zebra is not a component of the fire, but is obviously a piece of the strange zebra-fire entity. And by definition, any entity that engages in no such relation will be in a state of perfect sleep, perceiving nothing. While it may seem absurd that there could be entities without relation, do not forget the asymmetry of which we spoke: a thing is real insofar as it has qualities, and these entail pieces as their source. It need not have outward effects, which are always dispensable. The world is perhaps filled with countless entities that exist without any current impact, and which might never have any. While the fashionable doctrine today is that things are real only by virtue of having effects, in fact the reverse is true: they can have effects only because they are real.

Some objects do not relate for the moment, despite their descent from a probably endless chain of relations stretching back into the depths of time. Analogies can already be found in everyday life. For instance, every living creature has a long chain of ancestors before it, without this entailing that the creature itself will reproduce in turn. Another analogy would be that of a mythical sea with a surface but no ocean floor. In this case *some* water must always be positioned at the surface, even if it is different water at different times: droplets supported by fellow droplets beneath, and nothing but void above.

The remaining question is how an object shifts between states of sleep and wakefulness. It is not hard to see that an entity moves from one experience to the next by tunneling through its various perceptions into new ones. But how could the zebra choose to withdraw from objects into sleep, and later choose to resume its waking relations again? The answer is that it cannot. Like any object, the zebra simply is what it is without cease. But this means that entry into sleep, or re-entry into alertness, cannot be triggered by the zebra itself. Only the zebra's *pieces* are able to guide it into new situations of some kind. In other words, free will does not exist for objects, but only for pieces of those objects. In our own right we are cut off from the environment, but are partly at the mercy of our pieces. This is the strange converse of the principle that we always emerge beyond our pieces but do not always withdraw from outward relations. The infant exceeds its parents but is guided by them, not by itself; the parent is constantly immersed in the world of the child, but could easily have gone on living without that child. Concerning such issues of freedom and dependence, the usual choice is presented as follows. Either we exist within the world and are therefore determined by its mechanical laws, or we rise above it and are therefore free. Or perhaps it is said that we have both aspects at once, and are hence both free and not free without contradiction. But as usual the real situation is weirder than this, or even the reverse of this. Namely, by being withdrawn from the world as sleeping objects, we are *unfree* rather than free; being just what we are, we are incapable of anything else. Yet in a sense we are always *inside* the world through the fact that we are made of pieces— and only *therefore* are we free, with our components doing the work of liberty on our behalf. For there is an excess in our pieces beyond what is needed to create us, and this excess allows new and unexpected things to happen.

But the idea was strange, and the burgundy too strong in my blood to push it further. Again I turned to Latour's window to watch the storm. The hailstones struck the flag, yet the zebra continued to sleep. And so it is with all objects. We are awakened neither by our own powers nor by the world outside, but by the swarming landscape *within*: the pieces we never exhaust or master despite exceeding them. The dormant zebra, like all other objects, awaits a hailstorm from below.

Afterword

This book was written slowly, but published with surprising speed. The story of its publication began with a visit to a Chicago literary agent, a barrel-chested hustler with a reputation for shepherding unorthodox works into print. Acting on the advice of Professor Michael Witmore (Univ. of Wisconsin) I attended the meeting accompanied by my three most colorful friends: a surrealist, a Zen monk, and a telepath. The first was a foppish Belgian with a waxed moustache, generally clad in the smock of a mime and a corduroy hat, met by chance one summer at St. Xavier's tomb in Goa. The monk was a Japanese acquaintance (and my cousin by marriage) who had taught me the rudiments of meditation during a period of personal crisis. The telepath was a stranger hired for a ridiculous birthday prank some months earlier, but had performed so brilliantly on that occasion that he was quickly admitted to our closest circle of friends. On a late morning in February, we all trudged together through the slush of the South Loop to a structure designed by Burnham and Root themselves, and took the rickety elevator to one of the middle floors of the building. It was a Saturday afternoon; the hallways were empty, but the door we sought was already open.

The agent pointed needlessly to the armchairs and couches spread before his desk, and we were quickly seated. Chomping on a cigar, he glanced at the manila envelope under my arm and asked brusquely what it contained. After some hesitation and fumbling, I explained that it was a book of metaphysics in the long-abandoned style of Platonic myth, set in a decayed industrial infrastructure, and based on genuine stories from my travel diaries. The agent shook his head before my last sentence was finished: "I don't do metaphysics— no market. Anyway, Platonic myth has no future. And that infrastructure genre only works anymore for horror ... or pornography." He made the latter point with an unwelcome chuckle, but our innocent confusion on the topic left him troubled, and he continued in a more upstanding spirit: "I suppose this sort of thing could go over well in Central Europe, if you handled it just right. But not the American readership. And for travel books the market's always a bit saturated. But I'm not doing anything else, and it's wet outside. So let's hear it. What've you got?" My prepared response went roughly as follows:

"First is the description of a gigantic ferris wheel of many miles in diameter. It carries numerous objects in a long arc above the ground before sweeping them under the earth, past various chambers filled with objects ranging from the benign to the deadly. By considering the varied interplay between the objects in the wheel and the fixed entities that they pass, we are led to reject the present-day trend of abandoning individual substance in favor of events and relations. This imaginary wheel —mightiest monument in the history of the earth!— has great value for the philosophy of the twenty-first century. For through its example we are led to revive a metaphysics of objects.

"Second, I tell of an encounter with a dear friend in Annapolis shortly before her unexplained disappearance. Her philosophical position was of the Deleuze-Simondon variety, though the present book mentions this only in passing. More relevant here is the myth I invented to counter her objections. Spanning the Chesapeake Bay near Annapolis one finds a long and towering bridge, a marvel of engineering. My friend knew the bridge well enough: although a wealthy foreigner, she was born and raised within sight of it. Yet my story placed it in a context she could never have expected. Imagine numerous individuals standing on the bridge and throwing assorted objects into the bay, through emotional disturbance or some other reason. Imagine further that the bridge is transposed to the depths of Hell, where the legion of pre-Socratic thinkers is called upon to justify their theories in a series of rapid show trials, all of them failing and therefore punished by death. In this way my friend's metaphysical theories are gradually refuted, in favor of one where individual things regain their classical privilege, though in weirder form than the realisms of yesteryear.

"In Chapter Three I pay tribute to the odd Leibnizian doctrine of 'tiny animals': those minuscule bodies that remain attached to monads following the death of the visible creatures they animate. If we shift the image from animals to calliopes (or some other musical instrument) a myth takes shape to explain the fourfold structure of objects. But the choice of a calliope as my example was the work of chance: I simply happened to encounter such a machine one evening on the beach in Chennai, formerly known as Madras. And it was on that very day that I had been reflecting most seriously on the problems of Leibnizian metaphysics."

"Fourth, I find myself on a lonely offshore drilling platform in the Gulf of Mexico with a young English literary celebrity, through a series of events recounted briefly at the start of the chapter. In this desolate location, far from the mainland and in dangerous weather, I pass the time with my friend reflecting on three key features of causation, after some initial verbal sparring that I admit does credit to neither of us.

"The fifth chapter depicts a haunted boat. This story comes purely from imagination, without basis in my travels, except that it first came to mind on a ferry ride from Hiroshima to Matsuyama. Hence the myth has a strongly Japanese flavor. The example of the boat is used to explain my conception of 'allure,' in which objects are torn apart from their own qualities. In my theory allure is the basis not only of aesthetic experience, but of physical causation as well, though the myth can only hint at the full scope of the problem.

"In the final chapter, I recount a theory of relationless entities sparked by debate with the French philosopher Bruno Latour. The discussion occurred some years ago, just prior to a devastating hailstorm in Paris, and was interrupted early by outside factors. Taking slight liberties with chronology, the chapter incorporates my thoughts from a later period about what I call 'dormant objects.' The series of myths thereby comes to a close, and the outlines of a new metaphysical theory is thereby sketched, as proposed."

So far the agent had listened with a thoughtful attention that matched his reputation for mindfulness rather than his unspeakably sloppy appearance. But now came an ecstatic outburst from the man: "Jesus! That's a hell of a manuscript! What's the working title?" By prior arrangement the Belgian surrealist leaned forward, feigning contempt as he sneered: "Everyone knows... *Mustard*." The agent chomped a bit harder on his cigar, but otherwise looked perplexed.

All the while the telepath had been pressing his fingers to his temples, his eyes closed as if lost in some private inner vision. At once a loud crack resounded from the large cabinet in the room, startling the agent without ruffling those of us who had experienced such moments in the telepath's presence before. A few seconds later came another crack from the table, and then a louder but muffled burst from the floor near the center of the room. The rapid series of cracks then ceased, though the larger of the room's two windows began to rattle gently, and a faint whistling sound could be heard somewhere in the distance.

After a period of visible unease, the agent regained his composure and repeated his question concerning the manuscript's title. At this the Zen monk shouted a Japanese syllable, so meaningless in isolation that I do not record it here. This last gesture finally hit the mark. Whether enlightened by the shout or not, the agent began to laugh: softly and slowly at first, then coughing just a bit as he did so, gradually passing into increasingly heavy laughter, so that finally his face turned bright red. Wishing to encourage him, we all laughed along. After two or three minutes of uproarious mirth, the mood in the room returned to normal. Dropping his cigar stub into an antique ashcan, he practically shouted his next words: "Brilliant! You've got yourself an agent!" He then lumbered toward his computer as we all resumed laughing. The agent printed a contract, which I scanned lazily as he and the telepath gathered champagne glasses from a cabinet, while the Zen monk smiled and the surrealist took insolent drags from a hand-rolled clove cigarette. We still had no publisher, but the agent was known to be persuasive, and later events confirmed our assumption that the battle was already won.

Even now I recall fragments of sentences glimpsed in the contract through the half-drunken haze of that February afternoon: "... hereinafter called The Author ..."; "... shall receive the sum of $5,000 as an advance on ..."; "... in the event of the decease of any of the aforementioned parties, the arrangements shall ..."; "...hereby reserves the right to ..."; "... under the provisional title 'Mustard.'" Though the contract itself was later destroyed in a house fire, these phrases are etched forever in memory. But droll as the story may seem, I tell it with more than a touch of sadness: for three of the five parties to that conversation are now dead, two of them by natural causes. It is to their memory that this work is dedicated.

Notes

1 Alexis de Tocqueville, *Democracy in America*, p. 108. Translated by Arthur Goldhammer. (New York: Library of America, 2004.) The order of the passages has been reversed for reasons of literary effect.

2 Jostein Gaarder, *Sophie's World: A Novel About the History of Philosophy*. Translated by P. Møller. (New York: Farrar, Straus and Giroux: 1994.)

3 Aristotle, *Metaphysics*, Book IV, 1007b20-21. Translated by Joe Sachs. (Santa Fe, NM: Green Lion Press, 1999.)

4 Gilbert Simondon, *L'individuation à la lumière des notions de forme et d'information*, p. 51. Emphasis removed. (Grenoble: Millon, 2005.)

5 Thomas Metzinger, *Being No One: The Self-Model Theory of Subjectivity*. (Cambridge, MA: The MIT Press, 2004.)

6 *Monadology*, §72. In G.W. Leibniz, *Philosophical Essays*. Translated by R. Ariew & D. Garber, p. 222. (Indianapolis: Hackett, 1989.) Emphasis altered.

7 *Principles of Nature and Grace*, §3. In Ibid., p. 207.

8 *Principles of Nature and Grace*, §4. In Ibid., p. 208.

9 H.P. Lovecraft, "At the Mountains of Madness," p. 499. In *Tales*. (New York: Library of America, 2005.)

10 Michel Houellebecq, *H.P. Lovecraft: Against the World, Against Life*, p. 73. Translated by D. Khazeni. (San Francisco: Believer Books, 2005.)

11 See China Miéville, *Between Equal Rights: A Marxist Theory of International Law*. (Leiden: Brill, 2005.)

12 Reza Negarestani, *Cyclonopedia: complicity with anonymous materials*. (Melbourne: re.press, 2008.)

13 Edgar Allan Poe. *Poetry and Tales*, p. 1015. (New York: Library of America, 1984.)

14 Professor Bryant maintains the stimulating Larval Subjects blog at http://larvalsubjects.wordpress.com.

15 See Michael Ashkenazi, *Handbook of Japanese Mythology*, p. 227. (Santa Barbara, CA: ABC-CLIO, 2003.)

16 "The Principles of Philosophy, or, the Monadology." In G.W. Leibniz, *Philosophical Essays*.

17 Xavier Zubíri, *On Essence*. Translated by A.R. Caponigri. (Washington, The Catholic Univ. Press, 1980.)

18 Bruno Latour, "Why Has Critique Run Out of Steam? From Matters of Fact to Matters of Concern." *Critical Inquiry*, Vol. 30, pp. 225-248.

19 Peter Hallward, *Badiou: A Subject to Truth*. (Minneapolis: Univ. of Minnesota Press, 2003.)

20 The term "tool-being" appears nowhere in Heidegger: it was coined by my brother in 1992. See Graham Harman, *Tool-Being: Heidegger and the Metaphysics of Objects*. (Chicago: Open Court, 2002.)

21 See for instance Steven Shaviro, "The Actual Volcano: Whitehead, Harman, and the Problem of Relations." In *The Speculative Turn: Continental Materialism and Realism*, Levi Bryant, Nick Srnicek, and Graham Harman, Eds. (Melbourne: re.press, forthcoming 2010).

BOOKS

O is a symbol of the world, of oneness and unity. In different cultures it also means the "eye," symbolizing knowledge and insight. We aim to publish books that are accessible, constructive and that challenge accepted opinion, both that of academia and the "moral majority."

Our books are available in all good English language bookstores worldwide. If you don't see the book on the shelves ask the bookstore to order it for you, quoting the ISBN number and title. Alternatively you can order online (all major online retail sites carry our titles) or contact the distributor in the relevant country, listed on the copyright page.

See our website **www.o-books.net** for a full list of over 500 titles, growing by 100 a year.

And tune in to myspiritradio.com for our book review radio show, hosted by June-Elleni Laine, where you can listen to the authors discussing their books.

mySpiritRadio